HOW PERSONAL GROWTH AND TASK GROUPS WORK

SAGE HUMAN SERVICES GUIDES, VOLUME 55

SAGE HUMAN SERVICES GUIDES

a series of books edited by ARMAND LAUFFER and CHARLES D. GARVIN. Published in cooperation with the University of Michigan School of Social Work and other organizations.

1: **GRANTSMANSHIP** by Armand Lauffer (second edition)

2: **CREATING GROUPS** by Harvey J. Bertcher and Frank F. Maple

4: **SHARED DECISION MAKING** by Frank F. Maple

5: **VOLUNTEERS** by Armand Lauffer and Sarah Gorodezky with Jay Callahan and Carla Overberger

7: **FINDING FAMILIES** by Ann Hartman

10: **GROUP PARTICIPATION** by Harvey J. Bertcher

11: **BE ASSERTIVE** by Sandra Stone Sundel and Martin Sundel

12: **CHILDREN IN CRISIS** by Carmie Thrasher Cochrane and David Voit Myers

14: **NEEDS ASSESSMENT** by Keith A. Neuber with William T. Atkins, James A. Jacobson, and Nicholas A. Reuterman

15: **DEVELOPING CASEWORK SKILLS** by James A. Pippin

16: **MUTUAL HELP GROUPS** by Phyllis R. Silverman

17: **EFFECTIVE MEETINGS** by John E. Tropman

19: **USING MICROCOMPUTERS IN SOCIAL AGENCIES** by James B. Taylor

20: **CHANGING ORGANIZATIONS AND COMMUNITY PROGRAMS** by Jack Rothman, John L. Erlich, and Joseph G. Teresa

21: **MATCHING CLIENTS AND SERVICES** by R. Mark Mathews and Stephen B. Fawcett

22: **WORKING WITH CHILDREN** by Dana K. Lewis

23: **MAKING DESEGREGATION WORK** by Mark A. Chesler, Bunyan I. Brant, and James E. Crowfoot

24: **CHANGING THE SYSTEM** by Milan J. Dluhy

25: **HELPING WOMEN COPE WITH GRIEF** by Phyllis R. Silverman

26: **GETTING THE RESOURCES YOU NEED** by Armand Lauffer

27: **ORGANIZING FOR COMMUNITY ACTION** by Steve Burghardt

28: **AGENCIES WORKING TOGETHER** by Robert J. Rossi, Kevin J. Gilmartin, and Charles W. Dayton

29: **EVALUATING YOUR AGENCY'S PROGRAMS** by Michael J. Austin, Gary Cox, Naomi Gottlieb, J. David Hawkins, Jean M. Kruzich, and Ronald Rauch

30: **ASSESSMENT TOOLS** by Armand Lauffer

31: **UNDERSTANDING PROGRAM EVALUATION** by Leonard Rutman and George Mowbray

32: **UNDERSTANDING SOCIAL NETWORKS** by Lambert Maguire

33: **FAMILY ASSESSMENT** by Adele M. Holman

34: **THE ACCOUNTABLE AGENCY** by Reginald Carter

35: **SUPERVISION** by Eileen Gambrill and Theodore J. Stein

36: **BUILDING SUPPORT NETWORKS FOR THE ELDERLY** by David C. Biegel, Barbara K. Shore, and Elizabeth Gordon

37: **STRESS MANAGEMENT FOR HUMAN SERVICES** by Richard E. Farmer, Lynn Hunt Monahan, and Reinhold W. Hekeler

38: **FAMILY CAREGIVERS AND DEPENDENT ELDERLY** by Dianne Springer and Timothy H. Brubaker

39: **DESIGNING AND IMPLEMENTING PROCEDURES FOR HEALTH AND HUMAN SERVICES** by Morris Schaefer

40: **GROUP THERAPY WITH ALCOHOLICS** by Baruch Levine and Virginia Gallogly

41: **DYNAMIC INTERVIEWING** by Frank F. Maple

42: **THERAPEUTIC PRINCIPLES IN PRACTICE** by Herbert S. Strean

43: **CAREERS, COLLEAGUES, AND CONFLICTS** by Armand Lauffer

44: **PURCHASE OF SERVICE CONTRACTING** by Peter M. Kettner and Lawrence L. Martin

45: **TREATING ANXIETY DISORDERS** by Bruce A. Thyer

46: **TREATING ALCOHOLISM** by Norman K. Denzin

47: **WORKING UNDER THE SAFETY NET** by Steve Burghardt and Michael Fabricant

48: **MANAGING HUMAN SERVICES PERSONNEL** by Peter J. Pecora and Michael J. Austin

49: **IMPLEMENTING CHANGE IN SERVICE PROGRAMS** by Morris Schaefer

50: **PLANNING FOR RESEARCH** by Raymond M. Berger and Michael A. Patchner

51: **IMPLEMENTING THE RESEARCH PLAN** by Raymond M. Berger and Michael A. Patchner

52: **MANAGING CONFLICT** by Herb Bisno

53: **STRATEGIES FOR HELPING VICTIMS OF ELDER MISTREATMENT** by Risa S. Breckman and Ronald D. Adelman

54: **COMPUTERIZING YOUR AGENCY'S INFORMATION SYSTEM** by Denise E. Bronson, Donald C. Pelz, and Eileen Trzcinski

55: **How Personal Growth and Task Groups Work** by Robert K. Conyne

56: **Communication Basics for Human Service Professionals** by Elam Nunnally and Caryl Moy

57: **Communication Disorders in Aging** by Raymond H. Hull and Kathleen M. Griffin

A **SAGE** HUMAN SERVICES GUIDE **55**

HOW PERSONAL GROWTH AND TASK GROUPS WORK

Robert K. CONYNE

Published in cooperation with the University of Michigan School of Social Work

SAGE PUBLICATIONS
The Publishers of Professional Social Science
Newbury Park   London   New Delhi

For information address:

SAGE Publications, Inc.
2111 West Hillcrest Drive
Newbury Park, California 91320

SAGE Publications Ltd.
28 Banner Street
London EC1Y 8QE
England

SAGE Publications India Pvt. Ltd.
M-32 Market
Greater Kailash I
New Delhi 110 048 India

Printed in the United States of America

Library of Congress Cataloging-in-Publication Data

Conyne, Robert K.
      How personal growth and task groups work / by Robert K. Conyne.
            p.   . cm. — (Sage human services guides : v. 55)
      Bibliography: p.
      ISBN 0-8039-3340-1.
      1. Social groups.   2. Work groups.   3. Social group work.
      I. Title.   II. Series: Sage human services guides : v. 55.
      HM131.C7473   1989
      302.3—dc19   88-32686
                                                                                              CIP

FIRST PRINTING 1989

CONTENTS

Preface   9

PART I: A Task Group   11

1. The Committee on Social Responsibility Begins to
    Get Oriented   13

2. Susan Consults About Getting Oriented   19

3. The Committee on Social Responsibility
    Gets Organized   24

4. Susan Consults About "Getting Organized"   29

5. The Committee Produces Ideas   34

6. Susan Consults About "Data-Flow"   38

7. The Committee Problem-Solves   43

8. The Final Consultation: Problem Solving   51

PART II: A Personal Group   57

9. The "Personal Growth Group for Professionals"
    Begins and Experiences Dependency   59

10. Looking at Session One: Dependency   70

11. Real Conflict in the Group   77

12. Examining the Session of Conflict   82

13. Cohesion Begins to Emerge Around Bill   87

14. Processing the Cohesion Stage   92

15. Interdependence and Closure Emerge in the Group   97

16. Processing Interdependence   102

PART III: Conceptual Framework   107

17. Some Explanatory and Conceptual Supports   109

Annotated Bibliography   115

References   120

About the Author   121

This book is dedicated to my fellow group leaders,
group members, and students of groups.
May it prove useful.

PREFACE

This book is meant to provide a very practical approach to group work. I intend it to help improve both the understanding and the practice of this important helping strategy.

Two major forms of group work are considered:

— *task groups*, such as committees and planning groups, which are used by the thousands in this country to accomplish tangible goals; and
— *personal groups*, such as psychotherapy and personal growth groups, which are important vehicles for seeking individual change.

A significant difference between this book and the many others on the subject of group work is the approach to conveying knowledge. This book is built around two continuing stories, sort of short novelettes. One story is about a task group, called the "Committee on Social Responsibility," of a church. The second one is about a person group, called the "Personal Growth Group for Professionals."

This story device is used pedagogically to demonstrate how both task and personal groups may evolve, what can happen in them, and especially how their leaders and members perceive and experience these occurrences. This approach is from the "inside out," in a sense. The reader is led experientially to an understanding of group functioning and group development. Along the way, analytic chapters are interspersed, but these too are presented in a similar story-telling format. The final chapter of the book breaks from this format and is devoted to a discussion of the basic conceptual framework used in developing the groups. It is a group developmental life span approach suggested by Jones (1973) that I term the "task-personal stage" model.

Included following the treatment of both the task group and the personal group is a section called "Reflections and Activities." Here you will find an opportunity to engage more actively in the material just presented, so as to enhance and solidify your learning. To extend your learning, I have included at the end of the book an Annotated Bibliography. I hope the interested reader will turn to this section to acquire additional information about groups in general, or about personal and task groups in particular.

I think a very practical book such as this one can be useful for the wide variety of practitioners in social work, counseling, psychology, education, and the helping fields generally, who are using groups or who would like to begin using them. I see it as beneficial, also, as a supplementary book for basic group theory and process courses in these fields.

I am hopeful that the personalized account provided of these two groups will prove to be an interesting and informative way to explore group work for many. The characters you will encounter, from Reverend Bostow and Susan Sharp in the task group to Fred Sloan, Heather Smith-Harrelson, and Bill Johnson in the personal group, would like that very much.

—*Robert K. Conyne*

PART I

A Task Group

THE "COMMITTEE ON SOCIAL RESPONSIBILITY"

This first part of the book comprises eight chapters. These chapters will describe a task group. It is a committee in a church organized by its minister to better address social action in the community.

You will be introduced to Reverend Bostow and some of the committee members. You will be able to follow their activity in the task group, especially the development of the group leader (Reverend Bostow) as he becomes more effective in his role.

Consistent with the format of the book, the story of this task group will evolve according to progressive group developmental stages. For the task group, these are: Orientation (Chapter 1), Organization (Chapter 3), Data-Flow (Chapter 5), and problem solving (Chapter 7).

These chapters of the story alternate with a continuing analysis of what is occurring. In Chapters 2, 4, 6, and 8, you will see how a consultant to Reverend Bostow, a social worker named Susan Sharp, assists him to become a more knowledgeable and effective committee chair.

Finally, Chapter 17 in Part III defines the conceptual framework underlying the activities of this task group.

Chapter 1

THE COMMITTEE ON SOCIAL RESPONSIBILITY BEGINS TO GET ORIENTED

THE CONTEXT

The Church of the Brethren is located in one of the trendier areas of the city. It's not surprising, then, that its congregation is made up mostly of well-to-do, successful members. These people have either "made it," or are on the right track. Doing well—however that may be measured according to worldly standards—is a standard to which they had long ago become accustomed.

That's not to imply that these church members are totally consumed by their own life-style or smug about their status in life. Many volunteer for civic groups of various kinds or hold positions on major boards. Some are vigorously involved in local and state politics. All are in touch with the larger issues of the day, taking pride in their awareness of what is happening around them. But to Reverend Bostow, the minister of this church, this group of fine, well-polished people lacked a certain zeal for reaching out to others, especially those others who, in the lexicon of the Reagan presidency, were the "truly needy."

In fact, Reverend Bostow was plagued by what he considered to be his failure to move these upstanding church members to the kind of social service he deeply felt was absolutely necessary. Especially for religious people who were part of a church that had been long known for its endorsement of strong social policies in such areas as racism and discrimination, health and welfare, and peace. And even more especially for those religious people who themselves had "made it." To his way of thinking, these folks bore a special responsibility to reach out, to go the extra mile, to help those who could not really help themselves.

When he thought about this very much, Reverend Bostow found himself getting quite angry—at himself, more than at them. Why couldn't he light a fire under them? Why had he been unable to motivate them, to lead them, to help the countless poor, hungry, homeless, and destitute people of their city? What could he do?

What he had done over the four years he had been the minister at the Brethren was to increasingly use his sermons to inspire a kind of social gospel. Not every Sunday, certainly; that wouldn't have worked at all. But whenever he could take a message toward real-world, social involvement—and whenever it fit nicely within the scriptures—he would exhort. "Reach out." "Get involved." He would even give examples of where this could happen in their city—the Free Store, the Salvation Army, the Homeless Shelter. But he wasn't finding much change overall. In fact, he had met with some resistance to his notions. It went something like this: We are concerned, but we are also deeply involved with our own lives, families, careers. And, aside from that, religion is about spirituality not about social change.

Reverend Bostow was not a man to say no. Not without a whale of an effort. The only son of an immigrant farm family from northern Wisconsin, he was used to both hard work and meager resources. But he struggled, pulled himself up by his own bootstraps, as it were, to make something of himself. Into and through college, the first one not only in his family to do so, but also in his whole town of 200; working various odd jobs all the way to make ends meet. Into and through seminary, establishing a reputation for dogged determination as well as for a real concern for the "underprivileged." It was he, for instance, who organized fellow seminarians to volunteer their services at "Lighthouse," a runaway shelter in the inner city. He arrived at Church of the Brethren, after two positions at smaller churches, at the age of 32.

Eager and willing to assume this prestigious post, he gave it his all. And he was met with much goodwill. Attendance gradually increased, and many in the congregation talked of the new energy that seemed to take root there. In a very real sense, he felt as successful as his "charges." Both he and the church were "doing well" in nearly any way it could be assessed. Attendance, pledges, the youth group, the newly formed singles group, the physical facility itself, participation in churchly duties, how he was liked and admired by the congregation—all were in fine shape and, if anything, on the upswing.

Yet the reluctance of members to step outside themselves began to gnaw at him after about his third year at the Brethren. He was at a kind of crossroads with it now, feeling that all his efforts to sermonize about this had failed. Reverend Bostow felt that he must stimulate a deeper and wider kind of social responsibility in his congregation. He just didn't know how to do it.

That is, until his contact with Susan Sharp. Susan had moved to the city a year or so earlier to begin her work as a staff member at the Eastern Hills Community Mental Health Center. She was a social worker who specialized in group process, community organization, and consultation and training activities. She brought with her considerable experience working with a range of human service organizations, and she was especially adept at assisting in the development and maintenance of volunteer service efforts.

During her year in the city, Susan had been involved in different community organizing projects, including consulting at a Senior Citizens Center. There, she assisted the director in the design of a volunteer staffing program, and she conducted the first training sessions for the new recruits. The volunteer program was now established and was proving to be a useful part of the Senior Citizens Center operation.

Reverend Bostow was familiar with that center because his church was one of three in the community that contributed funds to help support the center's rent payments. Therefore, he made it his business to keep up with how the center was doing. It was in this way, during a conversation with the director, that he had learned of the successful new volunteer program that the center had instituted and of the Eastern Hills consultant who had been so helpful in its development.

The volunteer project sounded very exciting. In fact, Reverend Bostow recognized parallels between that project and the one he was attempting to get off the ground. As he thought about this after the conversation with the center's director, he decided to follow up with her to find out more about this consultant and how he might contact her at Eastern Hills.

The consultant's name was Susan Sharp. The director said Susan was about 30 or so, a social worker, in the city for around a year or so now, and that she was bright and extremely helpful and knowledgeable about organizing volunteer programs. Without Susan's help, she said, their volunteer program would still most likely be a vision floating around up there somewhere and nowhere near the very real program it had quite quickly become. The director strongly encouraged Reverend Bostow to contact Susan if the church had any sort of similar needs as she had had.

Buttressed by this information and support, Reverend Bostow called the Eastern Hills Community Mental Health Center and asked for Susan Sharp. After talking briefly by phone, they agreed to set an appointment for late the next afternoon to explore the issue in more depth.

Susan was curious about what this idea could be and looked forward to the meeting. She had not yet worked with a church, and she was interested in doing so. In her mind, some of the social action work that churches do in the community had always been impressive, even done by those churches that were located in affluent areas of the community, such as the Church of the Brethren. She wondered how—and if—she might be able to be helpful. For his part, Reverend Bostow was mulling over a new approach to getting congregation members more involved in the community—forming a committee, a kind of task force, to give shape to this activity and to guide its implementation. But this was somewhat foreign to him, not since his seminary days with Lighthouse had he undertaken such an activity. And, aside from that, his skills were not in this area of organizing and group work. He was a preacher, an inspirer, and sometimes a good listener. Maybe this is where Susan could help . . . .

And so they met. Susan listened to his idea and found it compelling, very much in the social service/social change tradition of much community work that she knew many churches had been involved with over the years. She agreed (as any community organizer would) that social and community involvement of this kind was desirable. She thought that a committee was a reasonable way to proceed. She also heard the uncertainty of Reverend Bostow below the surface in his presentation, as well as his obvious commitment to social justice.

Although she was already very busy with other projects, she decided quickly that she would like to be involved in this effort in some useful way. So when Reverend Bostow asked if she could work with him or the committee, she was pleased to agree. She suggested that, if he would like, she could assist him as a kind of "consultant." In such a role, she explained, although she would not normally be present in the group, she could help him periodically to plan its activities and to analyze what was happening, with the control and responsibility for it residing with him. Reverend Bostow recognized this approach as similar to how she had successfully worked with the Senior Citizens Center. He was eager for her assistance in any way, he said, and so they agreed on this direction.

And so he began, albeit somewhat impulsively, having not worked through with Susan how to go about the initial stages.

THE FIRST MEETING

The reverend invited eight members to attend the first meeting of the new "Committee on Social Responsibility." These were people with whom he had talked before about community involvement. They had seemed interested and supportive. Therefore, not knowing where else to start, he sent them a letter of invitation, a standard procedure in the church. All eight showed for the first meeting in the conference room.

It was a disaster. The conference room is dominated by a very beautiful, large teak table, undoubtedly priceless, the gift of a former church trustee. Committee members arrived for the meeting, seating themselves around this huge table. While most of them were prompt in their arrival, three straggled in after the 8:00 p.m. hour, the last person appearing—breathlessly—at 8:35.

The time from 8:00 to 8:35 seemed an eternity to Reverend Bostow. After all, he was used to giving sermons at the stroke of the hour to an assembled audience. There, everything was clear and orderly. But here, here was something else again. He wondered: Should I begin or should I wait for everyone to arrive? Should I introduce all of them? Do they all know one another? Should I tell a story to pass the time? We only have until 9:30, so perhaps I should move on. That's what he finally decided to do at 8:20.

In the meantime, while he was mulling over these thoughts and checking over his notes, the others sat silently or filled the time by talking quietly in two's or three's. Several glanced impatiently at their watches from time to time.

Reverend Bostow broke into this rather uncomfortable setting at 8:20 to "begin." Feeling the urgency of moving ahead, he thought it best to move directly to the heart of the matter, after first thanking them for agreeing to participate. He explained that he was forming this committee to bring before the congregation ways for them to get involved in the larger community of which the church was a part. He underlined the importance of this for religious people and for their church. He then began to expand on these items, talking nonstop for 20 minutes about some of his own ideas. His thoughts came out in torrents, as if a cork had been unplugged suddenly. They could write a manual, they could videotape some social service agencies, they could themselves volunteer and then report to the congregation about their experiences, they could survey agencies about their needs, they could spend time on the streets to get a better sense of the problem, they could . . . .

All this was brought to a halt upon the arrival of Frances DuShay, of the breathless entry. It seems her car had run out of gas some five blocks away. And she was determined to make sure that everyone was clear that she was not irresponsible, that she was very busy, that she was extremely interested in the committee, that she had worked on a similar committee (she thought) in a city where she used to live, and so on. For 15 minutes she apologized and explained, getting mostly support and "warm fuzzies" from the others, including Reverend Bostow.

Of course, it was now about 9:00, leaving 30 minutes until the meeting's end. Reverend Bostow suddenly became very aware of the time crunch, but he could not think—for the life of him—of a graceful way to move the attention from Frances to the task at hand. He was saved by George Fuller, who allowed that all this was important, he was sure, but he—for one—had to leave in 15 minutes to pick up his daughter from play rehearsal at school. What did Reverend Bostow want them to do?

Being saved is one thing and knowing what to do next is quite another. But Reverend Bostow seized the moment by asking the members to list what they could do to stimulate community involvement by church members. Now, he thought this was a very clear assignment. After all, he had already given some of his own ideas about this topic. And yet his request was met by deafening silence. He remembered thinking, quite painfully, that here is a group of high-powered, successful adults behaving as if they were in grade school all over again. Not volunteering ideas, staring at the floor, clearing their throats, shuffling in their chairs.

Reverend Bostow let this go for a couple of minutes, tried to encourage them again ("Any ideas will do just to get us started"), and then could stand it no longer. "What about my idea of some of us spending some time on the streets, getting to know more about what it's really like?" he asked. Which was received by raised eyebrows and wrinkled brows.

By now it was 9:15 and George excused himself, as promised, from the meeting. His leaving seemed to break the impasse, but not in a particularly productive way. It allowed the others to say, in various ways, that they had to leave a little early, too. All of them, it appeared, had immediately remembered that they just simply had to be somewhere else than here. The last few minutes of the first meeting, then, were spent in apologizing and leave-taking, with Reverend Bostow asking (maybe imploring) them to return next week at the same time. He felt terrible. And he knew this committee was on the ropes, if not down for the count already. He clung to the hope that Susan would help.

Chapter 2

SUSAN CONSULTS ABOUT GETTING ORIENTED

Reverend Bostow and Susan met two days later in his office. That was how they had planned it. Two days following a committee meeting the consultation session would be held. It was to last 30 minutes, which was all that Susan could possibly spare, with her hectic schedule at the university and the commute to and from the church. She recognized that this probably would not leave enough time to process the previous meeting thoroughly and to plan the next one, but it would just have to do; who knows, maybe it would work out fine, especially if the committee meetings went well.

Reverend Bostow had been on pins and needles ever since the first committee meeting. He had thought of calling Susan at the Mental Health Center to see if they could meet sooner, but had dismissed the urge. He really did not want to appear as shaken as he was about this whole thing, anyway. But, indeed, he was shaken, not to the core, maybe, but shaken fairly deeply nevertheless. How silly and juvenile, he thought. It was just a meeting!

He also retained hope that Susan would quickly be able to put him on the right track. There must be some simple, little thing I missed, he surmised. I'm so out of practice, he worried.

And so, with these thoughts running through their minds, they began the consultation session.

"How did it go?" asked Susan brightly (and hopefully) to kick off their discussion.

Not being sure how this would sound at all—weak? secure?—Reverend Bostow plunged ahead. "It was a nightmare. At least for me.

Nothing went as I had planned. I'm not at all used to 'bombing' but I may have this time."

This is probably not what a busy consultant hopes to hear. Susan wanted him to say something like, Marvelous! Everything went smoothly, people were involved and excited about being there, and I felt very comfortable. We got a lot accomplished and I know exactly how to proceed for the next meeting. But she also realized that just because her consultee was a minister was no guarantee of Nirvana. She suddenly determined that a lot of work was ahead of them.

Susan also knew that she needed some information in order to be helpful, and that Reverend Bostow was in real need of support. "It sounds like you had a rough time of it and that you are kind of reeling from it still. That happens quite often and it's difficult to handle. But maybe we can figure out how you can regain some confidence and direction. But, first, can you tell me what happened, starting at the beginning?"

He did just that. Seeing no sense at all in trying to make himself look better than he was, Reverend Bostow painted a realistic picture of the meeting, from the agonizing beginning to the sudden departures. Periodically, she would interject to ask for a clarification or to inquire about how he felt about something that had happened. Sometimes she asked him what he had wanted to accomplish by doing something; for instance, when he spoke nonstop for 20 minutes about what the members could do to get involved in the community. Mostly, she listened to what he said and to how he said it. Content and feelings were equally important.

"Reverend Bostow," she began. He interrupted to say, "Susan, I really don't feel like Reverend Bostow here. If you don't mind, why don't you call me John? I think that would help our working together on this."

"OK—John," she replied, trying to get used to the informality. "May I tell you what I've been hearing and then offer some suggestions?"

"Please do," John said, "And—please—be direct. I think I need some fast help."

This, of course, is a courageous request not usually seen in the beginning stages of a consultation. Consultees at that point are more frequently intent in preserving their image by appearing to be generally in control and competent. Susan was grateful for his openness and willingness to receive straight feedback and suggestions. She fully realized that a consultee's tendency to defend and protect is the biggest and most time-consuming part of consultation. More than a few times, it had doomed the whole effort.

So Susan shared her observations. "It sounds to me," she began, "that you so badly wanted the meeting to go well that you may have been pressing, trying to do too much yourself. So much so that the committee members were not given any space—any opportunity—to let you and each other know of their own thoughts and reactions."

John looked puzzled, and Susan wanted to check if her observations were at all accurate. So she drew from an incident that occurred in the committee meeting as a way to make the discussion more concrete.

"Remember when you explained why you formed the committee and then you gave them 20 minutes, I think you said, of ideas about how they could get involved? I see that as an illustration of how you may have been pressing, taking perhaps more responsibility than you should have, too early. Helping them to talk might be more effective. What do you think? Am I accurate in this? Does it make sense?"

"I see, now, clearly what I must have been doing wrong. I think I was falling back on being the minister—almost preaching to them—rather than making room for them to get involved. But why would I do that, and how can I correct it?" he asked.

And this is the pattern they established. John would describe a situation that occurred in the meeting and Susan would listen. She might ask questions to get the information she needed. Then, she would share her observations, maybe offer a suggestion, and be sure to check with John if she were on the right track. Sometimes she would ask him to try answering his own questions.

For instance, Susan responded to John's wondering why he "played the role of preacher" with "I have my hunches about it, but I'm not sure. Do you have any ideas, John?"

Sure enough, he did. And they came a little painfully. "I think it's real important to me to have all the answers," he began, somewhat tentatively. "I want to look like I know what I'm doing." This was coming more freely now. "After all, I am not only the minister here, but also the committee chair! And when a silence occurs, I seem to feel this need even more strongly, so I rush in with answers, direction, almost anything to keep it going. Yes, I can see this happening very clearly," he admitted, with a sense of satisfaction that often accompanies a sudden awareness, as if a light just switched on.

"That sounds really plausible," agreed Susan. "And I would even bet that the large, impressive conference table fits in to that all somehow, too. While it certainly is beautiful, for a small group like this one, where you are trying to get them all involved, the table may create unnecessary and counterproductive distance and, with you at its head, it may add to this need of yours to be in charge . . ."

"I never thought of it that way," mused John. "Maybe . . ."

"If so, it may be that you would want to minimize this need to be in charge and to take excessive responsibility; then not using the table for this meeting could become desirable. Maybe switching this meeting to a more informal setting might be a good idea, I don't know. What do you think?"

He liked that table and the conference room, too. They provided a kind of stability and seriousness that he found comforting somehow. Yet, now that Susan had mentioned it, 8 people (9, including him) seated around a table that had easily held 25 in the past did seem a bit out of place. And, another thing: He remembered that some people seemed to strain to see other people when they talked. That was probably due to the long rectangular shape of the table.

"I think you may be on to something there, Susan. And maybe even moving to another room could communicate a kind of new beginning. Let me think about that."

Susan had some other observations she thought were worth sharing. To do so, though, she had to revise her schedule in order to give her 15 more minutes to spend with John. She called Eastern Hills to do that, and then returned.

"John, a couple of more things before I go. The first half hour or so sounded quite uncomfortable for you, and maybe them, too. It might have been useful for them to be introduced in a relaxed way, affording them a more natural way to talk until the meeting began."

"And then, while I'm thinking of it, the whole matter of orientation is very important in initial meetings. Getting introduced to each other and to the task at hand—and then being given an opportunity to talk about these things. I don't think you provided for the kind of personal introductions I am speaking of (including of you and your interest in this area), but you did take a stab at laying out for them the purpose of the committee—which was very good, as I see it. It is my hunch, however, that much more time could have been spent here. *I call this orienting to people and to purpose.* Kind of who we are, what brings us here, what we may have to offer, and what this whole project is about. 'Getting the lay of the land' might be a colloquial way of saying it."

"Let me say one more thing about this, because I seem to be on a roll and time is short. I think you were so intent on getting down to business that you began to push much too early—before they really had much of an idea at all of what this committee was to do, and of how they would feel about participating in it—*for producing what I would call 'solutions' prior to understanding the problem.* You offered a bunch of solutions early, such as spending some time on the streets. Then, toward the end when you encountered a silence in response to what they could do to stimulate community involvement by church members, you asked them to generate a list. Why the silence? I think it may be because you were way ahead of them, asking them to give solutions and make commitments long before they were ready to do either."

"Now I've said a whole lot of things, without giving you a chance to respond, John. Sorry. What do you make of all this?"

Susan had hit the nail on the head so many times that John was suffering from overload. Too much, too accurate, too fast. But he also knew that this was exactly what the doctor ordered. Maybe this was going to work.

"I'm a bit stunned, Susan. You hit bull's-eyes every time. I don't know how I could have been so inconsiderate, so pushy. I feel like kicking myself."

"The important thing is not to punish yourself, of course, but to see what you might be able to do next time to do even better," corrected Susan. "While I am pleased that what I've said seems to ring true, I am a whole lot more interested in what might you do next."

This was difficult. But, of course, John keenly realized that he had to plan better for the next meeting.

"I'm not at all sure," admitted John, "but it seems that I need to provide some direction—some orientation, as you call it—and some real opportunity for them to participate. I may change where we meet to allow for more informality; the coffee room may be a good place. We didn't talk about how to handle latecomers or those who take up lots of time and attention, but I just think I'll be better able to respond to these kinds of unpredictable events next time.

"Susan, I thank you for your help here. I feel much better about all of this. And I'm sorry that we went overtime."

"I'm glad to be of whatever help I can," said Susan. You will be fine at this, I think. And about the time—we had best plan for 45 minutes in the future, don't you think? I'll rearrange my schedule to fit."

John nodded in agreement and was about to ask if she was sure that she could afford the additional time, when Susan went on.

"Finally," she said, as she put on her coat to leave, "sometimes you have to gently redirect the focus of attention to where you think it should be. In this case, Frances DuShay probably should have gotten less time than she did and maybe a little less support."

"But, speaking of time, I must leave to make my 11:00 meeting downtown. See you next week, same time, same place?"

Chapter 3

THE COMMITTEE ON
SOCIAL RESPONSIBILITY
GETS ORGANIZED

Next week had come. To Reverend Bostow, it seemed that the first committee meeting had taken place only yesterday, certainly not a week ago already. Sometimes it seems that the really good things in life come infrequently while the bad or difficult ones appear with great regularity. So it was in this case. Not that the committee meeting had been "bad." But it certainly had not been enjoyable or easy, and most likely not very successful. He imagined the members thought the same about it.

He very much wanted this unpleasant situation to improve. After his meeting with Susan, he had decided it might be necessary for him to take some risks to change it, in order to become a better organized committee. And, while he was aware of feeling anxious about the approaching meeting, at the same time he was feeling a sense of confidence about what he might do to better manage how things could go. He had listened closely to Susan's observations of the first meeting and he was intending to put as many of her suggestions into practice as he possibly could.

The first change he made was to move the meeting from the conference room to the coffee room. While he did this with reluctance, he recognized that the coffee room provided a smaller, more intimate feeling—and that this was the sort of feeling that might be more helpful. It was kind of the difference between a family room (or maybe even a kitchen) in a home and its larger and more formal living area.

This move also replaced the large rectangular teak table of the conference room, suitable to seat 20 or 25, with a round table that could accommodate up to 10 comfortably. When Reverend Bostow carefully placed nine chairs around the table, one for himself and for each of the committee members, he even more concretely grasped the change in the meeting place. In some ways, he thought, this much more informal and basic setting was more in keeping with the topic of concern for this committee: how to become more socially relevant in the community. He wondered what effect this physical change would have on committee members when they appeared for the second meeting and, more important, on how the committee would function. As for himself, he was aware that he would likely miss, at least at first, the comfort and security that the fine old teak table provided.

Reverend Bostow also intended to approach the next meeting differently. It had become clear to him that his anxiety for the first meeting had produced a kind of haste that prevented the natural participation of the members. This, then, blocked the committee from organizing itself to approach the task before it, the development of a community social action program. He needed to back off some, to let people get involved and to get oriented, as Susan had put it. Perhaps then they could begin together to produce some needed organization and direction. He was telling himself that he did not need to pressure himself to be the sole source of direction and guidance. Of course, putting this new line of thinking into action—beginning in 30 minutes at the second meeting—was his challenge.

Committee members were redirected to their new meeting place, in the coffee room, by a sign on the conference room door. Because it was just down the hallway, Reverend Bostow also found it easy to greet the members as they arrived and to walk with each one to the coffee room. Amazingly, to him, all eight of the committee members not only returned for this second meeting, but they were all pretty much on time (including Frances DuShay)!

Once they had all found a seat around the round table, Reverend Bostow opened the meeting. He began by commenting on the room change.

"I decided to try out a new meeting place for our committee meetings," he said, "because I thought that the big conference room kind of got in the way of our working together last time. While it's a wonderful room, and the teak table is absolutely gorgeous, I think it may be more appropriate for our business meetings—of which we have many, as some of you know only too well! Anyway, I wanted to experiment a little and see if this more cozy setting might work better. Besides, I somehow sense that this space here is more in line with discussions related to community involvement, which is why we are meeting together. But I am very curious about your impressions. What do you think?"

He recognized that this kind of approach was something that Susan would approve of. In fact, she had given him the idea. At the same time, he was aware that doing it felt risky. He felt vulnerable, somehow, opening himself up to the possibility of negative reaction and, worse, rejection. So he kind of held his breath as he waited for the committee members to respond to his question.

George Fuller had just sat in his seat. He was a busy man, the owner of a successful art gallery in the city, the father of three adolescents, and the husband of a real estate agent who was consistently a member of the "Three Million Dollar Club." He was also an active member of the church, serving over the years in a variety of leadership roles. So he tended to expect, if not to insist, that time be "well spent," focused on the task at hand.

At the same time, George was not an impatient man. He had learned over the years from his art gallery business the importance of attending to people, of giving them time, of not trying to force them to do things too quickly, or of not attempting to push them into making decisions too fast. And George was the first to respond to Reverend Bostow's question about the change in meeting rooms.

"Well, I've just sat down, so maybe it's too early to say. But right away I do tend to agree with you that this room is better suited to what we may do. And I think I really do like being able to see everybody here easily. Scattering the few of us around that big table—and, as an art gallery owner, I agree about its beauty—made it hard to see everyone. Let's go with it."

There were other comments from a couple of members, all of them positive, and head nods from everyone. And so the change was agreed to and supported, and Reverend Bostow felt validated and relieved.

Frances asked if she might pick up on a point that she thought was related to their different meeting place, and Reverend Bostow encouraged her to do so (even though he was beginning to worry that they were not yet getting "down to business").

Frances DuShay was one of those people who always seem to have many irons in the fire. Being late to the first meeting would not be atypical for her, nor would double-booking appointments. She was extremely active in a variety of volunteer commitments in the city and had become involved in the church only six months or so before. Although Frances tended toward the impulsive side, she was also a very able contributor to the large number of projects she involved herself with and was certainly not shy in making her viewpoints known.

"The point George made a few minutes ago about being able to see each other easier now reminded me of two things. And I am a little hesitant to mention them, but I will anyway," she laughed, and barged ahead. "First, I must confess that I don't know the names of everyone here. It's probably because I'm pretty new here and, most likely, all of you know everyone else. Second," as she turned to Reverend Bostow directly to address him, "how would you prefer us to call you here? Reverend Bostow seems a bit formal, I don't know . . ."

Boom! The directness of Frances's comments hit Reverend Bostow squarely in his stomach. He felt a kind of panic almost. All at once he realized that last week's meeting must have been far worse than he had suspected. In his haste to "get going," he had not even allowed the committee members to introduce themselves! And, just as bad, he had not let them know—and perhaps he had not faced this yet himself—how he would like to be addressed here!

Reverend Bostow now faced a dilemma. Should he try calmly to recognize this need to introduce one another and then quickly to move on to the tasks at hand, or should he respond at a deeper and more personal level? Based on Susan's consultation with him, he decided, again with considerable trepidation, to take the latter tack.

"Frances, I thank you for saying what you just did. Frankly, I'm disappointed in myself for not taking care to be sure we all knew each other. I think we should spend some time on that. And, please feel free to call me what is comfortable for you, for all of you—John would be perfectly fine as far as I am concerned."

"Let me go on. I think there may have been some other things I could have done a little better last time. At least, I want to mention them and see what you think. I think it's really important, if our committee is going to be productive, for everyone to have a good opportunity to become involved and for us to have a free and open exchange of ideas. Otherwise, we may never get organized enough to work on our task. Frankly, I have been kicking myself around a little since our first meeting because I am convinced I didn't do that. I did not give you a chance to talk much, to get involved and say much what you thought. I did most of the talking and that did not seem to work well. Maybe tonight we can change that. I think I want to ask you for your contributions, to kind of freewheel it some, and I might do better for a while by listening and helping us to guide some of the stuff that comes out of this process. That's not to say that I might not enter in, too, but I do think that my involvement—and yours—can become more effective. Well, all that's a real mouthful, and I'm anxious about how you are reacting. What do you think?"

Maybe it's that church members don't usually expect their ministers and priests to openly admit to making mistakes, that is, to being human. Just as likely, members of most committees look to their leaders for direction and, especially in the early stages of committee life, accord them with more power and infallibility than is justified. Whatever the reasons, these committee members—even the impulsive Frances—were taken aback by Reverend Bostow's admissions and his completely different style this week as compared to last. The immediate response, then, was a predictable (and uncomfortable) silence, lasting about 10 seconds, followed by George's comments.

"You know," began George, "it's only 8:30 and already I think we have probably accomplished more—in just 15 minutes or so—than we did the entire first meeting! That's my overriding thought right now. As I was driving over here tonight I was really wondering if I would continue with this assignment. I am being candid here. But I am feeling a huge change now. We do need to get organized. And John—how's that—the changes are due to you, I think, because it seems to me, at least, that you are putting your finger on some things that are important to do here."

"I agree!" exclaimed Frances, with great enthusiasm. "Why don't we begin all that by introducing ourselves and getting to know each other just a little bit. And, if you don't mind, Reverend Bostow, I would also like to call you John here."

Others commented, too, all agreeing in one way or another with George and Frances. The remainder of this second meeting was devoted to getting organized, the task that Susan Sharp had advised John as being necessary to address.

Committee members took turns introducing themselves. Each was invited to say a few things about their lives, including the nature of their interest in community involvement and any ideas they might have of how their committee could proceed. John Bostow also followed suit. By engaging in this exercise, which ended up consuming the rest of the meeting time, John thought in retrospect that two really important outcomes were realized. The first, and more obvious one, was that everyone now knew some things of interest about every one else on the committee. It now seemed that people could connect a little bit better. Second, and this was a big and somewhat surprising result, many ideas about community participation came out of this sharing! The committee was beginning to create a kind of agenda of possibilities, it seemed.

As compared to his dismal feelings about the first meeting, John was elated about how this second one went. He couldn't wait until the next meeting! And he couldn't wait to tell Susan about the successes that occurred!

Chapter 4

SUSAN CONSULTS ABOUT
GETTING ORGANIZED

"The contrast between the second and first meetings was like day and night," John enthusiastically began the second consultation session with Susan. "I must admit—I feel more than a little pleased with the difference. In fact, I would really like it if all the meetings could go as well. You'll have to forgive me a little, Susan, for crowing some here!"

"No, not at all," reassured Susan. "It's just as important and useful to acknowledge the good times as the more difficult ones and you have every right to feel good. I'm glad you're able to express that—and that the last meeting went so well. Tell me, what was it that allowed all those good things to occur?"

About this, John wasn't so sure. He hadn't taken the time to analyze reasons for the difference. Somehow he was aware of wanting to stay away from that, as if analyzing why it occurred might destroy the fact that it did, or that it might remove from him his feelings of pleasure. He also knew that identifying whatever reasons he could would be useful for future meetings.

"You know, Susan, I am really not altogether sure of that. It really didn't seem that I did a whole lot, but things were much improved. I don't know . . .," he repeated as his voice trailed off.

Susan sensed some resistance to her question. Sometimes, she had discovered, consultees would unconsciously block exploration for a number of reasons—the material was too painful, they did not trust the consultant, they wanted to hold on to a positive experience and not examine it, or whatever. She decided to check the possibility of resistance here.

"John, I noticed a real difference in your responses so far today. You seemed very excited when you told me about the last meeting. But when I asked you for possible reasons about why it went so well, your affect rather suddenly became more subdued and distant. I'm wondering if you might not want to probe this, that you might just want to leave it alone?"

Why was Susan always right about these things, he wondered? Yes, of course, this was what was going on, plus his interest—underneath it all—to find out.

"No, you're right, Susan," he said. "I do and I don't, I think. I don't know if that makes any sense, but I feel quite mixed about this. Almost as if I don't want to spoil a good thing. But, in spite of that, I do want to find out more about why that meeting went so well. Let's move on!"

So Susan listened to John's account of the second meeting. How he had changed the meeting place and how members seemed to respond so well to that. How Frances had asked about getting acquainted and about how she could address him. And as he related this event and how he had responded, John remembered how anxious he had been in trying to decide what to do then. He recalled feeling something like a small panic. The very idea of his not making sure that everyone in the meeting had become acquainted still was upsetting to him. And his decision to admit to them his disappointment with his own participation in the previous week's meeting had only added fuel to that fire.

"I think that whole area, around the question of Frances and what my options were then, really was uncertain for me," he said to Susan. "I felt challenged, maybe even a little attacked, and didn't know what I should do."

"One of the better ways of evaluating if a particular course of action was positive or not is to assess what happened immediately afterward," offered Susan. "What did happen after you did what you did—I mean, after encouraging the introductions, giving them permission to call you what they wanted, and then after you self-disclosed about your involvement last week?"

"The rest of the meeting was great," exclaimed John, with his enthusiasm returning. "In fact, people participated so actively that it wasn't necessary for me to do much after that. Maybe that's where my feeling of really not doing much in that meeting came from."

"Let's wait about that last point of your's, but let's not lose it either," said Susan. "By your account, what you did do appeared to promote your goals. That is, a more relaxed atmosphere in the meeting was established and members began to interact—it sounds—with a lot of energy. They became involved with each other and, to your surprise, with the task. That sounds wonderful, and a complete turnaround from the first meeting! You were helping the committee to *get organized*, just as we had discussed at our last session together."

"Now, what is it that helps explain those positive changes?" she asked.

"Maybe I could take a stab at this and see what you make of it," John agreed.

"Contrary to your inclination, John, I think you did a whole lot in that second meeting. A whole lot that was positive. You recognized the need for a more informal and relaxed meeting place, acted on it, and asked members for their reactions. By doing this, you demonstrated that you were concerned about the committee and about providing the most suitable place for it to meet. You took action, but you evaluated it through obtaining their initial reactions. And it worked, that's the best part of it!"

Susan continued. "While that took some risk on your part, what you did next, I think, took a gigantic risk! No wonder you were feeling some sort of 'panic.' Of course, I'm referring to the incident, and I would say, the *critical incident* that occurred when Frances put you on the spot. That's what she did, she put you on the spot by a direct and pretty brave couple of questions. She took a risk and it placed a demand on you. The question for you was, 'what should I do?'"

"I think this was critical," said Susan, "because of its immediacy, you had to do something right then, and because of the choice points you had available to you. My guess is that your tendency would be to provide the opportunity for a brief response but then to get back to the 'task at hand,' back 'to work,' as it were. But you chose otherwise in this case and I think it paid off royally. You sanctioned getting acquainted and, much more than that, you succeeded in cracking the ice to reveal a concern that not only you had but the rest of them did, too: The first meeting had not gone well, it had been unrewarding, and you had had a hand in that. What a risky—there's that word again—and helpful admission on the part of a leader! And you can see the positive effect it had."

"Yes," broke in John, "I remember a silence that seemed like an eternity—no religious meaning intended!"

"Oh, sure," responded Susan soothingly, as if a silence at that point might be completely natural and expected. "This kind of self-disclosure by you, by the minister who usually might not come across in that way, was unexpected and it surprised them, I would bet. They probably needed that time to gather themselves."

"But what happened after that, as I understand it, is that you got nothing but agreement and support, followed by virtual nonstop participation. Not only at a personal, get-acquainted level, but also at the level of generating ideas about involvement in the community. I think you were able to provide an atmosphere that allowed them to get involved, and that set all of you on the way to organizing for the task. It's ironic, that by acknowledging and supporting personal contact and expression among the members, and by doing this yourself, the members were encouraged to become much more involved with the task. Isn't that what you wanted to happen?" asked Susan.

"Yes, certainly," agreed John. "I am beginning to see that what I did may have led to the better meeting. That's exciting!"

"Yes, it is, very exciting," said Susan. "And an important part of that is generalizing what you did to future meetings of this committee. That is, being able to continue doing these new things."

"I couldn't agree more," John quickly responded. "Which brings up the issue of the next meeting. I have been so enthralled with the second meeting that I haven't even thought about the next one. What do you suggest?"

Although Susan was reluctant to offer direct suggestions, preferring to guide the consultee in generating them, she chose to respond directly as the time was slipping by quickly.

"Two main points come to mind," began Susan with her suggestions for the next committee meeting. "The first is to be a little bit cautious of the unanimous good feeling that characterized your last meeting. While it feels very good right now, and everyone is reveling in goodwill, you can most likely expect some conflict to occur by the next meeting or two. In fact, until this conflict is expressed and dealt with somehow, it may very well be that the 'high' being experienced now might really be more artificial than substantive. I don't mean to deflate or to minimize its importance; but I do want to tip you off that it will need to be tested through conflict of some sort, and that you can naturally look for this to happen soon."

"The second point that occurs to me," continued Susan, "is that while the sudden rush of ideas that was generated was very positive, there is now a need to become more 'tasky.' This is addressing what you had brought up a little earlier, and I had said to hold on to it, that we would get back to it. You were concerned with your not doing much during the meeting. Well, what you did do helped members to begin getting properly organized. Things were going so well that it was not necessary for you to continue doing a lot—except maybe to listen and to encourage. But now that many ideas have been offered, it is time to provide assistance in developing them."

"I'm wondering," Susan went on, "what was done with all those ideas? For instance, were any of them recorded?"

John admitted that they were not; he had been so caught up in what was happening that writing down the ideas had completely slipped his mind.

Susan offered, then, that the next meeting could easily pick up with the ideas that had been produced. They could go back to that point and begin to list the ideas on newsprint. Susan likened this process to a kind of brainstorming, but this time being sure to record everything very quickly, with no evaluation of individual ideas. Maybe they could do that in 15 minutes or so, and then spend the rest of the meeting discussing the ideas, leading eventually—perhaps in the following meeting—to selecting which idea or ideas they would want to pursue seriously.

John wondered about his role in this process, and Susan suggested that he think of himself as a guide or as a facilitator of the process. With regard to next meeting, she thought it might be very useful for him to propose the activities for the meeting, to take charge of the newsprint listing, to attempt to stimulate ideas, and then to guide or facilitate a discussion of each one. The overall goal might be for him to further enable the organizing process of the committee. He could help committee members to generate alternatives, to discuss them, to decide, and then to put them into action. She went further, by proposing that John develop a tentative agenda for the committee, an agenda that might be organized according to the program development process steps she had just discussed. She had anticipated this turn to their consultation and had brought with her a copy of a practical guidebook for program development and evaluation for John to read. But, she emphasized, the focus for the next committee meeting should be on more systematically identifying ideas for community involvement and then discussion of them. Once at the discussion point, Susan said the committee would be engaging in a stage called "*data-flow.*"

This had been a very full consultation session. They had covered lots of important material, ranging from an analysis of the last committee meeting to plans for the next one. Susan felt strongly that John was moving along very productively and that he had greatly aided the committee to become better organized to accomplish its goals. So did John, but he thought that getting ready for the third committee meeting would take some doing. It seemed quite complex, as he considered it. Why, he even had homework!

Chapter 5

THE COMMITTEE PRODUCES IDEAS

As John thought about Susan's words during the week, he was most concerned about the potential conflict she had mentioned. While he supposed she was right about it (she had certainly missed on nothing yet), he was hard-pressed to imagine what this conflict could be or where it could come from. He also was aware that conflict was something he was uncomfortable with and he fretted about how he would respond.

The program development and evaluation guidebook was helpful. After looking it over, he had a better idea of doing what Susan suggested was important for the upcoming meeting—producing ideas and getting them recorded for decisions. He remembered she had called this "data-flow," a sort of strange term, he thought. John liked the idea of using newsprint to record the many ideas that members had about community involvement, and decided that was what he would do.

And so the third meeting of the committee began. John welcomed everyone and went straight to work. He was very focused and was totally ready to move ahead directly from the last meeting.

He explained that what they needed to do now was to begin capturing all of their excellent ideas on newsprint so they would have a record. Later, they would refer to this record as they sought to choose an approach for community involvement. He also explained that the process they would follow would be a modified form of brainstorming. He would ask them to quickly list a number of ideas that came to their minds, without taking the opportunity then to discuss them or to evaluate their quality or practicality. Those steps would follow.

Throughout all this, which took only 10 minutes or so, John felt self-assured and confident. He was well-prepared, having been introduced to this approach by Susan and then having read the guidebook. He knew where to go and pretty much how to get there.

After his brief presentation of how they would proceed, he began the brainstorming enthusiastically with "Let's begin!"

No one began. John waited, at first stunned by the lack of response. He looked around the table. Committee members, instead of appearing eager to participate, seemed to be avoiding it. They reminded him of a school class, with students doodling or looking suddenly for a dropped pencil; and he was the hapless teacher, left hanging. And very uncomfortable.

For Frances, this high-energy, high-focus beginning by John was just too much. She was still worrying about her Aunt Sarah, who, Frances just two hours ago learned, had fallen and broken her hip. Frances had rushed over to the hospital to see her, grabbed a quick sandwich in the cafeteria, and just made it here for the meeting with no time to spare. While she was remembering the excitement of the last meeting, jumping into tonight so suddenly and directly was simply not working.

George was having problems, too, but for a different reason. Although he had participated actively in the previous week's meeting and felt good about all the ideas that had been generated, during the week he had become concerned about this church actually putting any of those ideas into practice. He knew the people in the church pretty well, he thought, having been so active in it for so long. The church's record on social action in the community was not impressive, in his judgment. So since the last meeting he had begun to wonder if the committee should consider this issue before going very much further. But now John was really pushing ahead, as if he were oblivious, or unconcerned, about their actually getting something done. George was struggling with what to do.

John felt caught. After all, this wasn't how things were supposed to go right now. The silence that met his invitation to begin, it seemed to him, had now reached the millennium mark.

John broke it, after about a minute. Attempting to press on, he rephrased the task for the evening, this time adding something about time to be spent on it and reinforcing the notion that this approach would really be helpful to them as they thought through what would be best to do. This time, he asked if they were ready to begin?

Still, a silence. A shuffling of feet. An avoidance of eye contact. A few throats clearing and pens tapping.

By now, John felt perspiration under his arms. He was very aware of struggling to right this reeling ship, of finding the right words to use.

When he was about to restate the task for the third time, John impulsively decided against that and to simply find out what was going on.

"Wow," exhaled John, "this isn't at all like last week! I'm not sure what is happening. Aren't you ready to go ahead?"

This yielded something.

"Yeah," began George, "I'm not sure about going right ahead. I don't think I'm ready to do what you want me—us—to do, John. After I thought about it since our last meeting, truthfully I wonder if our church is at the point where a lot of these ideas could ever get backing, I mean get enough people to participate in them, in order to do them? One of my ideas, for instance, of restoring an abandoned apartment for low-income housing, sounds good, but would we be able to get anyone to actually do the needed nitty-gritty work?"

Others then took turns responding to John's question. Frances explained how she just wasn't, maybe isn't, ready to pick right up where the committee left off last week because of her preoccupation with her aunt's situation. Remaining members also mentioned hesitancies, due to a variety of reasons.

Hearing these, John realized at once that the committee was at a point of conflict. This is the sort of thing, he recalled, that Susan had alerted him to expect at some point. Now he was feeling a bit relieved because he could label what was occurring and he could place it within the realm of "normality." By doing this, John found some direction.

"Well, perhaps we should lay off the newsprint for now and talk about some of the things you are concerned with. We can always go back to listing ideas, and so on, later. How does that sound to you?" inquired John.

The discussion that followed for the next 45 minutes was enlightening. It became clearer to John about why the committee members did not charge directly ahead with his proposed way of proceeding. Simply put, he and they were at far different places tonight! And, as important, they were able to talk candidly about the commitment of their church to community projects. This proved to be extremely helpful for all of them, as it allowed them all to better understand the context within which they were working. It also enabled John to express his own dissatisfaction with what he saw as the church's poor track record in this area. They agreed that whatever they would come up with in terms of a community involvement project would need to have a high chance of endorsement from as many church members as possible. They decided that this issue would be important to consider later as they evaluated whatever ideas they were to generate.

When it seemed that they had completed this discussion, John asked if they were now ready to move on to the task he had proposed at the start? Now, they all agreed, they were ready.

And, indeed they were! In a way similar to last week, the committee members generated a list of 10 ideas for potential projects. These ideas included the apartment restoration, developing a volunteer outreach program to shut-ins, beginning a program for young fathers, becoming involved in the "Community Coalition for Social Justice," linking interested church members with the Eastern Area Community Center to provide a range of services to the poor, sponsoring a continuing series of workshops on selected issues of social justice, instituting a church study group on world peace, conducting fund-raising for one of the shelters for homeless people in the inner city, establishing a Church Community Counseling Center for the needy, and holding regular food and clothing drives among church members for distribution to the needy, among others.

This didn't take much prompting by John at all. He was more than busy just trying to keep up with listing these ideas on newsprint, and with forestalling the natural tendency of people in situations like this to want to explain their idea or to ask questions about someone else's.

The difference between this week and last, of course, was that now there was a recorded listing of ideas. Just as important, the committee had surfaced issues that demanded examination, and they had resolved them—at least for the moment.

That was the "good" side. The "bad" side was that only 15 minutes remained for discussion and analysis of these 10 ideas! Realizing this time constraint, John made note of it to the committee members and suggested that they hold off their discussion until next meeting, when they (he hoped) could devote considerable time to discussion and to problem solving. He then suggested that they spend the last few minutes reflecting on how things were going in the committee.

"How do you think we are doing here?" he asked bravely.

What he got was—what seemed to be—honestly positive reactions. They felt movement in their working together and, when they got stuck, as they did tonight, they felt good about being able to get unstuck. They seemed to feel that something was going to come of this, something that they—and the church—could be proud of and that would make a difference for people.

John left the meeting with a warm glow.

Chapter 6

SUSAN CONSULTS ABOUT "DATA-FLOW"

"This was the best, and maybe the most difficult time so far," John said to Susan to begin their follow-up consultation of the third committee meeting. "I was—and am still—simply amazed at all that happened."

This caught Susan's attention. She asked John to fill her in on what had happened, suspecting that somewhere in the presentation the issue of group conflict would appear. John launched into his description with ease.

As she listened, Susan was impressed with the increasing confidence and sophistication that John showed regarding group dynamics. He was capable of not only describing well what had occurred in the meetings, but, more often than not, he was able to analyze correctly why these things happened the way they did. He was even becoming skilled at identifying what leader interventions would be helpful—that is, what he did or could do—to further committee movement. Of course, his advancements made the job of consulting much easier, too.

John's account, then, took on much less the form of asking Susan for her explanations of what had happened, or of soliciting her advice about what to do. Now, John was beginning to turn to himself for explanations and for direction. As long as accuracy and competence are demonstrated, this flipping of the frame of reference from an external orientation (the consultant) to an internal one (self) is a hallmark of professional development.

And so Susan was recognizing that the quality of their working relationship seemed to be evolving from that of the "expert" consultant working with the "novice" consultee to a much more collegial one. She was excited about that development, because empowerment of the consultee is a principal goal in consultation. At the same time, she was somewhat taken aback at the quick pace of John's progression; it reflected well on his ability to comprehend and to apply new learnings.

"One of the most helpful things for me," said John about the third meeting, "was remembering what you said about anticipating conflict sometime soon. I think that once I was able to recall that, when we hit some rough spots during the meeting, I was then much more adequate at handling it."

Susan recognized the importance of being able to hang events on conceptual hooks. That is why she had tried to prepare John for the upcoming conflict that she knew, based on how committees and other groups develop over time, was bound to happen. Being able to label in one's own mind something that occurs as expected, or within the range of normal development, all of a sudden can transform a perception of the event from that of chaos, for instance, to one of predictability. And, therefore, the event—in this case, conflict—falls within the reach of being managed.

"Yes," Susan agreed. "Having a reasonable idea of what to expect can be reassuring. How did it help guide what you did or didn't do?"

"Well," reflected John, "I think at first I really didn't remember it. I mean, all during the week before the meeting this issue of impending conflict was on my mind almost constantly, it seemed! But when, in the meeting, it was staring me in the face—you know, when absolutely no one would volunteer ideas—it completely slipped my mind. I remember feeling very alone and totally at a loss about what to do to get them going. I was very much intent on *moving them along*, I certainly remember that very clearly. In your words, I guess, I was trying very hard to produce the "data-flow" that we had begun toward the end of the week before. And I was really struggling to find a way—maybe if I rephrase my invitation, maybe I wasn't being clear, I thought—that this would then allow them to participate. After all, *I* was really primed to get going. I assumed they were, too. But, I learned I was off-base with that belief."

"So your effort to push them along did not yield any fruit, is that right?" asked Susan. After John nodded agreement, Susan inquired, "What did you do that worked so well?"

"I don't know, really," admitted John. "I simply, for some unknown reason, kind of blurted out that things were not going well here and I wondered what was going on—or something like that," offered John. "And the incredible thing is that right afterward—I mean immediately afterward—people began to explain what was holding them back. I was astounded!"

"What do you make of that, John?" asked Susan.

"I think I blundered into an effective strategy, maybe," John said. "It reminds me of the time in the second meeting when I was trying to press them, to move people on to working before they were ready or—I'm still somewhat horrified about this—before some of them even knew each other's names. I 'backed off' then from the task and it seemed to work. I think maybe the same kind of thing happened again. I backed off from pushing on the task to find out what was in the way of working on it right then. And I found out! Some people, like Frances, were just caught up in some of their own personal matters and found it difficult to jump right in and George introduced the whole issue of what sort of social justice projects were actually doable in our church, given our less than stellar history in this regard. All of this was extremely useful and as we were discussing these things, it hit me—kind of after the fact, but I did realize it—that we had been at a conflict point, we were working at it, and it was OK. That was a marvelous realization."

"That makes sense to me, John, very good sense," offered Susan supportively. "I think it could be that you have identified a dynamic about how you work in meetings that may be important for the future. What I'm thinking of is that you seem to have a tendency to push 'ever onward' on the task at hand, when the members may not be ready, for whatever reasons. This, we have seen now at least twice, has led to a blockage in productivity. You have been able to free up the blockage both times by moving right away from the pushing on task to a completely different mode: asking them what they would like to do now, or asking them what is in the way. Something like that, anyway. The results have been that members have become involved once again with the task, in a direct and energetic way. It seems almost paradoxical. Removing work pressure, at times, can lead to improved work flow . . ."

John concurred. "I think you're right, Susan. And I want to remember that about myself. Certainly, it helped to move us through the conflict we were facing and we generated a lot of great ideas! The energy level became really high and I had all I could do to just keep up with writing down all the ideas that people produced—10 of them. But, then, that brings me to another couple of points. The first is that after the ideas were out, we were almost out of time, with only about 15 minutes remaining. My decision was to hold off discussion then and, rather, to reflect on how the committee was functioning. This felt kind of strange to do, but once again, it seemed to be very effective! The second point is that now that there are all of these ideas, I'm not sure how to work with them at the next meeting."

"Let's take those two points one at a time," replied Susan, as she glanced at her watch and noticed that just 15 minutes remained for this consultation session. "Regarding the first one, my mother had a favorite expression: 'The proof is in the pudding.' It worked! And, I think, with good reason. Many experts advocate leaving time at the end of every meeting—maybe 10 to 15 minutes—to evaluate and discuss how well the group is doing. Sometimes even brief evaluation forms can be circulated and completed, and then used as the basis for discussion. The idea is that building into the ongoing practice of the committee or work group direct attention to evaluation—and then using the results to help shape future activity—represents an important method to keep the group on track and functioning effectively and efficiently. You picked this up almost intuitively, it seems, and used it successfully at the end of the last meeting. Bravo! You may want to consider incorporating this approach into every meeting, or every third meeting, or some such schedule, to assure that evaluation is occurring and that members are given an opportunity to provide feedback.

"With regard to your concern about how to manage all those ideas," Susan continued, "it seems like another chapter in the guidebook will be useful. I encourage you to read it, because it is very practical and straightforward. But, generally, you probably want to be concerned with the overall question of *feasibility* for each of the ideas that were presented. Probably before you get to that issue, you will want the 'author' of each idea to present it briefly and then for the committee to engage in a short discussion of each. Remember, no discussion has yet occurred, just a simple listing of ideas. Then, after people have a pretty good understanding of these ideas, they will then be in a position to evaluate their feasibility. By this I mean how doable are they in your context? Actually, it sounds as if George raised some feasibility questions already. When you look at the guidebook you will notice a technique called *force-field analysis*, which allows you to examine forces that might support the accomplishment of the idea, compared with forces that might hinder its accomplishment. Take a good look at that, it can be helpful to use. Other ways of determining feasibility include asking questions about the *appropriateness* of the idea—is it something that the church should be doing; the *adequacy* of the idea—can it help to make a reasonable difference in reducing the problem; the *effectiveness* and *efficiency* of the idea—can it reach desired goals in an affordable way; and the potential positive and negative *side effects* that could occur as an unintended consequence of the idea's implementation. Of course, these kinds of feasibility questions about the ideas need to be raised with a clear, shared understanding of what your *goal* is. Maybe that would be the place to begin, to be sure you have agreement—that you have consensus about what it is you expect to accomplish.

"What you will be engaging in," continued Susan, "is *problem solving*. You now have progressed through a series of developmental steps in your committee, from orientation, to organization, to data-flow, and now to problem solving. This last step may take some time because you have so much data. In fact, I recommend that you plan for spending two meetings devoted to discussing and analyzing the ideas. You may find that some of them can be discarded fairly quickly because they are obviously too ambitious, or just wouldn't work in your setting. By using the criteria I have touched on here, and that you'll read about in the guidebook, you'll finally winnow the list down to a smaller, more workable number, I suspect. And then your committee should find itself in a position to make a decision. One last word of advice, though. Remain sensitive to issues we have spent a lot of time on as you proceed—such things as attending to conflict and how members are interacting—as you proceed with the problem-solving steps."

With that, the consultation time was up for that session. They agreed to meet after the next two sessions, in large part because Susan needed to be at a conference the next week. And John once again realized that he had more homework awaiting him. However, although Susan had presented a lot of information very quickly at the end of the session, this time he also felt a sense of confidence that had not been present before.

Chapter 7

THE COMMITTEE PROBLEM-SOLVES

As John prepared for the next step, which Susan had referred to as "problem solving," his confidence grew even stronger. The guidebook material on problem solving was specific and concrete; he was finding tasks outlined in a systematic manner, and this was very appealing to him. At the same time, John was keenly aware of Susan's injunction that he remain sensitive to his tendency to push ahead without giving appropriate attention to how people might be feeling. The positive difference now, though, was that he was aware of that dynamic, for he had confronted it now several times. He felt certain that he could avoid falling into that trap again; or, if he did (which was probably more realistic), that he would be able to correct it.

The fact that two meetings would pass before he would meet with Susan again did not particularly bother him, either. In a very real sense, John was feeling that his abilities to lead this committee were becoming apparent. He felt much more "grounded" in his skills, with a self-assurance in these matters that—although it was quite new—nonetheless seemed authentic. He also sensed that Susan shared this positive estimation of his competency, which bolstered his conviction even more.

As a means of facilitating the committee's problem-solving efforts, John decided to follow the advice contained in the guidebook by preparing a problem-solving grid. This grid could be used by the committee members to aid in their consideration of the 10 alternatives that they had already generated. It occurred to him as well that providing a framework of this kind on paper might also allow him more of an opportunity to attend to the human relations issues in the committee. He made special note of the caution expressed in the guidebook: "Offer the grid as an aid, but use it only if the committee members support it."

He hoped they would endorse using the grid. Its steps seemed so logical and potentially useful. He liked their flow: Identify the problem, state the goal, generate alternative strategies to reach the objectives, analyze each of the alternatives by using force-field analysis and feasibility criteria of appropriateness, adequacy, effectiveness, efficiency, and side effects, and then deciding by consensus. Beyond that, the guidebook presented other major steps for implementation of the selected alternative, followed by how to determine if the implemented alternative was successful in reaching the established goal.

John determined that the committee had already progressed to the step of analyzing the alternative strategies. He saw the next two meetings as dealing with their analysis and ending with a consensus decision about which one they would select. His grid, then, took care of that much of the process. He knew that subsequent meetings would address the next critical steps of the problem-solving process: preparing for implementation and evaluation. But those would be for the near future.

So he prepared his grid as follows:

ANALYZING ALTERNATIVES AND SELECTING A STRATEGY: A WORKSHEET

Problem: Our church is not involved with programs in our community to help promote social justice. This represents a moral failure and an abrogation of what is one of our missions.

Committee Goal: To implement at least one social justice program in our community that would be supported by most congregation members.

Alternatives: [Here he abbreviated in a list each of the 10 alternative strategies that had been developed by the committee:]

#1: Start apartment restoration project

#2: Start shut-in outreach program

#3: Start young father program

#4: Community Coalition for Social Justice involvement

#5: Eastern Area Community Center involvement

#6: Start workshop series on social justice

#7: Start study group on world peace

#8: Start homeless shelter fund-raising

#9: Start church Community Counseling Center for needy

#10: Start food and clothing drives

Analysis:

ALTERNATIVES

1 2 3 4 5 6 7 8 9 10

CRITERIA

_____

_____

Supports

_____

Hindrances

_____

Appropriateness

_____

Adequacy

_____

Effectiveness

_____

Efficiency

_____

Side Effects

_____

_____

Discussion and Consensus Decision

_____

_____

John liked this grid. He was especially fond of the force-field analysis approach for weighing the supports for and constraints on each alternative. He could envision examining at least some of the alternatives quite systematically through this technique. He worked up a "Force-Field Analysis Worksheet," also, for just this purpose. John included an example of a supportive force and a hindering force for the second alternative the committee had generated, "Start shut-in program," just to show how this technique might work. The Force-Field Analysis Worksheet looked like this:

FORCE-FIELD ANALYSIS WORKSHEET

COMMITTEE GOAL

"To implement at least one social justice program in our community that would be supported by most congregation members."

INDIVIDUAL ALTERNATIVES

For example, Alternative 2: "Start Shut-in Outreach Program"

SUPPORTIVE FORCES	HINDERING FORCES
Eg., "We already have a small shut-in program for Bible study"	Eg., "Getting people to work in that volunteer program has proven to be difficult"

The overall Grid and the Force-Field Analysis Worksheet provided an organization, a framework, for problem solving, that he thought would be very helpful. Yet, based on previous experience and on the advice of both Susan and the guidebook, he recognized the necessity of checking out the committee members' feelings about their use before moving ahead.

So at the start of the fourth meeting, he did just that. John introduced the concept of problem solving and indicated that this was where the committee was now in its work.

He said, "As I have thought about it during the week, I can see us spending maybe the next couple of meetings considering the 10 different alternatives we have suggested, and then deciding together which one we want to pursue. Of course, following that decision, I guess we would move into planning how to put that alternative into effect, but that would come a little later."

He paused, and asked, "Does that make sense to you?"

He received several head nods.

"OK, then," he went on, "assuming you also saw it this way, which I think you do, I then thought I would offer a general kind of plan that we might consider following to aid us in considering these alternatives and in reaching a decision. I have worked out a plan, which I have to show you, and to discuss. How does that sound?" he inquired of the committee members.

Frances quickly and enthusiastically responded. "Oh, wonderful, John! I'm really glad you have a plan for us to look at, because there are so many ideas that this is pretty overwhelming—at least to me!" she admitted, with a sigh.

Others agreed. All of them appeared interested in looking at his plan for action. He even sensed some relief in them about it.

Feeling definite support to proceed, John passed out the grid and worksheet he had developed. As each member followed along, John then briefly explained the various steps contained on the grid, what was meant by each of the criteria, and how the Force-Field Analysis Worksheet could be used to weigh each alternative. He asked if all the alternatives that had been generated were listed and if he had captured them accurately in his abbreviations. He pointed out that, in his opinion, the committee had moved past the first two steps contained on the worksheet, called "problem" and "goal," and he asked them to look closely at how he had defined them.

"These are my understandings of the problem and goal that we are attempting to address here," John clarified. "Note that I included in the goal statement a reference to doing something that would be supported by most of our church members, which is something I think we have implied but I'm not sure we have been explicit about. But I, at least, have come to believe it's really important and that doing anything without broad support would probably be doomed to failure. Do any of you disagree or see the problem or goal very much differently?" he invited.

"I think you're right, John, about limiting our goal to what would be generally supported by our people," offered George. "On the other hand, how do we decide that? How do we know what would be supported? I have a feeling, too, that restricting ourselves in that way will lead us almost automatically to eliminating some of the ideas that were proposed . . . I'm not sure I like that part of it very much. But I still think you're right."

"I hadn't thought about how we might know exactly what would be supported," John said. "Perhaps we should discuss that now. What do you think about it?" he asked the committee.

Actually, they had begun to engage informally in a general force-field analysis of what supports and barriers existed in their church with regard to social justice efforts. After a short but productive discussion, they came to a conclusion that was somewhat painful, and that verified George's apprehension.

"It sounds," summarized John, "like we see the members of this church supporting an effort of this kind that is relatively low risk, low demand right now and that anything more might be perceived by them as excessive."

"Yes, I reluctantly think so," agreed George. "But," he quickly offered, "can we also see our first effort as the beginning step of a series of things we might do into the future? That would be much more tolerable and encouraging to me!"

The backing for George's suggestion was immediate and unanimous! And so the goal statement was modified to read: "To implement at least one social justice program in our community that would be supported by most congregation members *and that this program would be the first in a series of such programs.*"

With that important modification, the committee members, to a person, said that they were pleased with the grid and worksheet and were ready to move ahead.

John suggested that they move ahead by looking at the 10 alternatives in relation to the goal they had just agreed to.

"Are there alternatives that we could agree are perhaps beyond hope of achieving broad support for right now?" he inquired.

The ensuing discussion resulted in surprisingly quick consensus. Alternatives 1 (apartment restoration), 3 (starting a young father program), and 9 (starting a church counseling center) were all seen as being too ambitious for right now, and alternative 7 was dismissed because it addressed world issues rather than a more defined community one. It helped that committee members could see that these ideas, although perhaps inappropriate for right now, could become very desirable later.

The winnowing of those four alternatives left six for active consideration: Alternative 2 (shut-in outreach), 4 (involvement with the Community Coalition), 5 (involvement with the Community Center), 6 (sponsoring a workshop series), 8 (fund-raising for a homeless shelter), and 10 (running food and clothing drives).

As the meeting time was nearly expended, John asked the committee members if they might be willing to spend some individual time during the week considering each of the remaining alternatives in relation to the criteria for analysis contained on the grid, and to give particular attention to the Force-Field Analysis Worksheet.

He gave an example, this one different from the one he had presented on the worksheet. "For instance, take alternative 4, becoming involved in the Community Coalition for Social Justice. What supports and hindrances might be present? Could you each develop some specific information about those forces, to help evaluate the potential that an alternative actually may have for success? Then you might move on, beyond supports and hindrances to other considerations on the grid. How appropriate might that be for our church and in relation to our goal? How adequately would that kind of involvement meet our goal? And so forth, for the rest of the criteria. I think if each of us thought through some of these issues before the next meeting, we would have a good head start for it. What do you think?"

Everyone agreed, and the fourth meeting ended with direction and high energy.

Meeting five was held one week later, as planned. Members had come prepared. Some had even completed John's grid and had systematically worked through a few of the alternatives using the Force-Field Analysis Worksheet! Motivation was high among the members as they moved through the process of evaluating the six alternatives.

Following their analysis, consensus-seeking was quite straightforward and relatively painless. While each of the alternatives was deemed generally feasible and attractive, the committee opted for first implementing the "Workshop Series on Social Justice." They especially liked its potential as an agenda-setting and consciousness-raising vehicle for the church. That is, they viewed the series as offering a kind of umbrella under which a wide range of social justice issues could be considered—and brought to the attention of not only the community but, significantly, to the congregation members themselves. The series format also fit into the ongoing pattern of church activities, which regularly included seminars, workshops, and study groups on various religious themes. And, finally, the series was something they could control and direct and use to try to build broader involvement throughout its evolution. It seemed to all of them like a very good place to start.

John and the committee members felt good at the end of meeting five. They had arrived at a consensus about what to do, and with high energy. They were ready to continue on toward implementation. And John had a success story for Susan, too.

Chapter 8

THE FINAL CONSULTATION: PROBLEM SOLVING

It had now been a little more than two weeks since Susan had last met with John. As she was driving to the church for the next meeting with him, Susan recalled the plan that two committee meetings were to have occurred during that time period. She was excited to hear how they went and where the committee found itself now. Her sense was, and remained, that John had progressed markedly in his meeting-leading abilities. Consequently, she had seen his confidence surge ahead. Although certainly anything can happen, she fully expected that John would have a good "tale" to tell.

She was not to be disappointed! John relayed the events of the past two committee meetings assuredly, and with no small amount of pleasure. The committee was moving, that much was absolutely clear! And John seemed able to explain why. Susan was quickly surmising from this that John's need for additional consultation in meeting-leading skills was rapidly waning, if not over, at least for now. He appeared to have made substantial progress.

The way that John saw it—and he had done a lot of thinking about this in anticipation of this consultation session—the last two committee meetings had succeeded due to several reasons. As he had thought about it, the main theme running through all of them was that the committee had been *prepared* to achieve. By this John meant that, in looking back, he had noticed a foundation being built, an underpinning upon which a problem-solving method—maybe even any reputable problem-solving method—could build effectively. Here, he referred to the previous efforts in the committee to help members to get oriented to one another and to become acquainted with the task at hand. Then, moving on, helping the committee to get organized, to begin to establish a way to get work done and to be able to recognize and handle conflict. He mentioned the importance of drawing from the members their own ideas about what to do, of producing the flow of data that would be necessary for making decisions. He talked about the important lesson he had learned, more than once, of balancing attention to task and productivity with a focus on how members were feeling and what they were ready to do just then. And he concluded that all of these things—and most likely more—seemed to him to be building blocks in a foundation that could support arriving at quality decisions.

He went on, at Susan's urging, to share more of his impressions.

"And, then, the problem-solving method that you referred me to really worked well!" John said to Susan. "When you first described it to me the steps seemed overwhelming, but as I read about the method in the guidebook, they began to make very good sense. They were so practical and I really liked the way they built upon one another so nicely."

"What I did was to develop a planning grid and a worksheet for using force-field analysis on the alternatives," John continued. "Here, I brought you a copy," he said, as he handed Susan the materials.   "I passed them out to the members," John picked up the story. "But I passed the sheets out after—and I think this is crucial—*after* I had introduced them and their purpose tentatively. I asked the members if they would be interested in taking a look at a possible framework for us to use in sorting through the ten alternatives that we had generated. I tried to check this all out first, rather than laying it on them and telling them 'this is what we are going to do.' As it turns out, they were interested, I think they were relieved that I had something to propose and that I was checking it out with them first. Probably both of those. It worked! Your mother would be proud, Susan—you know, 'the proof's in the pudding!'"

"Yes, she would be!" laughed Susan. "Your committee has made tremendous progress, John. And this worksheet looks like it could be very useful. Good job! Is there any more to tell me?"

"Well, we wound up the last meeting with a decision on which alternative to attempt. I don't know if I really thought beforehand that we would get there or not. But we did, and everyone seemed to feel very good about it! We decided to develop the idea of offering the Workshop Series on Social Justice."

"Fabulous!" exclaimed Susan. "What allowed that to happen, do you think?"

"The preparation I have already mentioned. The steps of this problem-solving method were extremely helpful, I'm sure. And I think before we really got into those steps we discussed the goal for our work. You know, I had taken a stab at defining both the goal and the problem we were addressing by myself. But I thought they should have a chance to look at those and we could discuss modifications they might like to make. The whole notion of attempting something that would fit where our congregation is now with social justice involvement became important for us to consider and, from that, we developed an understanding that maybe for now we should start 'small' but see our first project as the beginning of several involvements in the future. Even as I think about this now, Susan, getting all of this clarified was probably very significant in allowing us to move productively forward. Actually, once we did that, we were pretty quickly able to reduce the list of ten alternatives to one of six."

"I see, I think," tried Susan. "Together you further defined the focus, or the goal, of your work. And you did that in relation to what would be supported by the church. Is that it?"

"Yes," said John. "I thought, and so did the committee as we discussed it, that attempting anything more initially would probably botch up the entire effort."

"'Pride goeth before a fall,' I know," said John. "And I hope I'm not being prideful or boastful. The committee is going so well and I am so excited about its prospects that I don't want to go off the deep end here! And I certainly know that I am not at all solely responsible for this turn of events; that will certainly help me stay humble! Susan, you have been incredibly helpful to me in this. I have absolutely no doubt that, without your expert consultation, this committee would be floundering today or maybe even disbanded. Susan, I want to thank you very much for your great help here."

"Thanks, John. Actually I just provided a few nudges and the work was done by you. And very swiftly, I might add! Rarely have I seen such progress. You have done a great job, and I think you have well in hand a sense of what you did to produce the positive changes; that's really essential for the future."

"But, I am beginning to notice that we are talking much more now in the past tense," observed Susan. "I mean, it seems to me that although your work with this committee—and with other ones in the future—is not yet over, it may be that we both are recognizing that your need for continued consultation now may be finished. At least I am thinking this may be so. What do you think, John?"

"Well, I feel a little bit shy about saying so, really, but I think you are right," agreed John. "I feel much more at ease and confident about how to approach this whole thing. I believe I am ready to go it alone on this one."

"Then, let's make it happen," offered Susan. "I think you are, too. I have enjoyed working with you, John, and I'm certain you will do well in this area. Let me know sometime down the road how things are going."

"Thanks, Susan, I will."

And so, after a little more winding down and friendly words, the consultation ended. John, the Reverend Bostow, continued to work successfully with the Committee on Social Responsibility (as well as other committees). And the Church of the Brethren, in turn, successfully implemented its Workshop Series. In fact, it would prove to be the precursor of a long line of future projects in social justice. Susan saw this happen at a distance, and was pleased.

REFLECTIONS AND ACTIVITIES:
TASK GROUP

The material that immediately follows is meant for students or trainees who are reading this book as part of a larger educational experience, such as an academic course or a workshop. Of course, other readers—such as practitioners—may find the questions and activities interesting and perhaps useful, too.

1. Form a small group of your peers. Choose a leader. Conduct a discussion session for 15 minutes about this topic: "The three best ideas I got from reading this section on the church committee were . . ."

2. Why is it that Reverend Bostow was having trouble with leading the committee effectively?

3. What are some important steps in a problem-solving method and how can they be useful to working with task groups?

4. Have you ever been in the role of a meeting chairperson? If so, how have you felt? If not, how do you imagine you would feel? Hold a discussion about this with a peer.

5. What do you suppose you would do if, as a chairperson of a committee, members failed to go along with your suggestions? Or, if you have been in this situation, what has been your experience? Can you relate to Reverend Bostow's experiences with this?

6. How important do you think the physical setting is for conducting effective meetings? What kind of setting do you feel is most comfortable for group activity such as was described in this section?

7. See if you can recall the group developmental stages that the church committee went through? Clarify those stages by talking with a partner.

8. Cite some advantages for a task group leader knowing something about group developmental stages.

9. Susan Sharp seemed to assist Reverend Bostow in his work. What was her unique contribution, do you think? "Being your own consultant" is a useful concept to consider. Do you see how you might be able to incorporate some of Susan's perspective into your work with groups in the future?

10. How effective a task group leader do you think you are right now? Do you see any ways that you might become more effective? Discuss this in a small group of your peers.

PART II

A Personal Group

THE "PERSONAL GROWTH GROUP FOR PROFESSIONALS"

This section of the book describes a personal group. Fred Sloan and Heather Smith-Harrelson are Licensed Professional Counselors who provide a personal growth group for professionals through a local YMCA. You will follow its development from their perspective and from that of one of its central members, Bill Johnson.

The evolving story of this group is organized according to the group developmental stages of dependency (Chapter 9), conflict (Chapter 11), cohesion (Chapter 13), and interdependence (Chapter 15). As with the task group format, the group events are analyzed and processed by Heather and Fred. They meet as coleaders for this purpose, which you will read about in Chapters 10, 12, 14, and 16.

Finally, Chapter 17 in Part III presents the basic conceptual underpinnings for this group and its progression.

Chapter 9

THE "PERSONAL GROWTH GROUP FOR PROFESSIONALS" BEGINS AND EXPERIENCES DEPENDENCY

THE CONTEXT

THE GROUP POSSIBILITY EMERGES

Heather Smith-Harrelson and Fred Sloan are Licensed Professional Counselors who have been engaged in a joint private practice for about one year. They each see a fairly wide range of clientele, from the unemployed automobile line worker, of whom there are many in the community, to the high-powered career executive interested in career change or caught up in a midlife crisis of some sort. In addition, Heather's case load includes a number of women who are concerned with a variety of women's issues, ranging from personal identity, to sexual identity, to battering.

Economically speaking, their practice is doing well enough to easily make ends meet. It is not doing well enough, however, for them to be comfortable and secure. They frequently joke, in a black, gallows kind of humor, about where the next dollar will come from and wonder if they will be out on the street tomorrow.

As well, Fred and Heather are frustrated that they have been unsuccessful in their attempts to form any counseling groups. If they had a waiting list (which they did not), they thought perhaps that would provide one way for them to form a group. They had sent a letter of invitation to selected "gatekeepers" in the community, such as lawyers, doctors, and religious leaders, seeking referrals for group work, but to no avail. And they had spoken occasionally to civic groups about mental health topics of interest, usually finding some way also to describe their group services, but nothing substantial had come of those efforts, either.

This was frustrating to them for two reasons: First, they value group delivery as an important form of counseling and they both have had considerable training and past experience in leading groups; and for economic reasons, offering groups would generate some of the additional income they need to better support their private practice.

Heather was a member of the local YMCA. In fact, she had met its executive director, Dave Hoover, through participating on the Y's annual fund-raising campaign. In talking with Dave, she had learned that the Y was interested in expanding its services to include offerings on "personal growth." Hoover was considering developing a personal growth program of workshops and sessions that would address such matters as personal finance, career development, human sexuality, and assertiveness training. Further, he was planning to contract out the provision of these kinds of personal growth services to qualified professionals in the community.

Armed with this new information, Heather and Fred began discussing the possibility of expressing interest in this opportunity. They saw it as potentially providing the means they were looking for to enable them to offer groups, assuming they were successful in landing the contract.

So Heather and Fred followed up with Dave Hoover and, to make a long story short, applied for a contract for offering a "Personal Growth Group for Professionals" through the Y. This process involved an interview with Dave about the needs of the Y and the experience and credentials in mental health and group work that Fred and Heather provided. They were then asked to submit a brief proposal which Dave would review, along with his executive committee. Two weeks later, Heather and Fred received a contract for offering the group during the Spring Quarter, which was five weeks away. Heather and Fred were to colead the group, while the Y provided the meeting space and marketing. As well, both the Y and the group leaders were to share in fees generated.

A POTENTIAL GROUP MEMBER

Bill Johnson would later become a member of this new group. Bill was a successful young lawyer. Now 30 years old, he had joined what was easily the most prestigious law firm in the city five years ago and had seemed to be on the fast track to a partnership. In addition to being very bright—Bill had received his law degree from Harvard—he possessed the right combination of smarts and education not only to do well, but to excel at the very highest levels.

On top of that, and this helped separate him from many of his peers, he had been more than willing to work hard and long hours at his craft, being fully aware that a partnership did not come easily. And, yes, he was more than a little ambitious. His eyes were dead-set on not only becoming a partner but on becoming a wealthy man. You may know the type: If he couldn't be a millionaire by age 30, certainly then by 35! The last time he had looked at his score sheet, about six months ago, he was pretty much on schedule.

Despite his career dedication, Bill was always able—somehow—to make room for women in his life. This was no "early to bed and early to rise" nerd. Early to rise, yes, he would qualify there, what with being at the office by 6:45 each day. But early to bed? Almost never, his work and his social life saw to that. His was a classic case of burning the candle at both ends, and managing not to get even slightly singed. In fact, there seemed to be a kind of boost he got from that life-style. He took pride in being what he thought of, typically immodestly, as an "All American Superman."

There was no one woman in his life and hadn't been since Chelsea Naismith, who was a Junior at Wellesley when he was a second-year law student. They had gotten really serious, fast, and Bill had proposed during the next year. Engaged, they were to be married following their graduation. But, tragically, her life had been snuffed out two weeks before the wedding. A semi jackknifed into her car on the Mass. Pike as she was driving home from a family visit to finish last-minute wedding plans, killing her instantly.

Although he was immediately devastated by this loss, Bill seemed to rebound swiftly. He tried to put the tragedy behind him by taking a position as far away from Boston as possible. His West Coast location and the outstanding firm he was associated with provided him at first with the escape he so badly required. He buried his loss and turned his full attention to his career, which began moving along at a rapid clip.

And soon he was able to resume dating. But never in the same way. He would see to that. No commitments, no continuing relationships. No risk. Good times, or "GTs," as he frivolously labeled them, were his compulsion. And he had lots and lots of GTs during the last four years, with some of the city's most alluring, single, career women. It had been only in the last year that he had consciously begun to be more careful in his sexual relationships, knowing what he did about the very real dangers posed by the many varieties of STD, particularly herpes and AIDS.

Maybe it was this newfound caution, born out of the fear of disease, that initiated the period of introspection—rare for him—followed by nothing less than the flat-out angst that shrouded his every breath today. The "All American Superman" image, that of the millionaire partner with all the "GTs" any man could ever possibly enjoy, was eroding. Slipping away, ever so gradually, as sand falls inexorably through an hourglass. He could feel it happening, almost as if his strength—maybe his very essence—were being bled from him. He was weakening, and to his own mind, fast becoming a mere mortal, with no special abilities, drive, or ambitions.

And the external signs of this dissipation were all too clear, at least to him. Now he was going to the office, like everyone else it seemed, between 8:00 and 9:00. The number of new accounts and billings—indeed, always a hallmark of his—was falling. And he had not been with a woman in two weeks; worse yet, he had little interest in changing that.

All this had been building for the last three or four months, he remembered. He could think of nothing special that set it off. It just seemed to accumulate like all so much old junk in the basement until—voilà—he hit what felt like rock bottom. Listless, empty, uncertain of what to do, Bill was barely going through the motions. He hated it and had never known anything like this in his life.

That's when he began to consider what he could do to get himself turned around somehow. He remembered back to the two or three career counseling sessions he had when he was a sophomore at Colgate. That seemed like an eternity ago now, but it was only 11 years. They had helped orient him to law as a field and that certainly had worked well. At least until recently. Yes, counseling was probably something he needed, even though he did not want to admit to it.

But where does one find good counseling? For Bill, that also meant easily and secretly, without colleagues and others knowing.

He nearly stumbled over the chance. As a longtime member of the YMCA, he was skimming the quarterly listings of recreational opportunities to see which he should register for the next morning. The Y was trying out a new set of offerings, explained the executive director in his introductory column. These personal growth opportunities would be provided for the first time this quarter and monitored for their participation levels. Bill turned to the new section on personal growth and there it was in black and white! A couple of professional counselors were offering a "Personal Growth Group for Professionals." This might be just what he was searching for . . .

PLANNING THE GROUP AND MEMBER SELECTION

Heather and Fred had the personal growth group for professionals all ready to go. Working together to produce a group design is always a challenge. For many coleaders, it is the most difficult part of group leading. Although they had yet to lead this group, Fred and Heather couldn't imagine that to be any more demanding than its planning.

Even though they had already developed the general framework for the group in their proposal to Dave, many important questions remained to be mutually decided: For instance, for whom was this group most appropriate, what would be the group goals, generally what would happen during each session, what would be each leader's responsibilities, what screening mechanisms would be used, how could they best inform prospective group members about the group and about their own qualifications for providing it, and how would the group be evaluated for effectiveness? This was very difficult work for any coleaders, and especially so for those who have not yet led groups together.

Fred and Heather found this planning and preparation at once burdensome and inspiring. Not only was finding the time to devote to this task a problem, given the ongoing business of their private practice, but coming to a satisfactory agreement about important points sometimes seemed impossible! For instance, Heather favored a fairly structured group experience, one that contained a number of planned exercises that were paced well developmentally. Fred, on the other hand, thought that structure inhibited the spontaneity of group participants and short-circuited necessary group dynamics; he pushed for a largely unstructured group. On this issue, but certainly not on all of them, Fred had prevailed.

It would not be fair to say that they fought about their differing views. But their planning sessions were marked by a large amount of conflict and high spirit, not about each other's capabilities, but about what the ideal group plan for this kind of group should contain. To their credit, Heather and Fred worked with and through this conflict to produce a plan that they felt good about in all ways. They had tested each other, tussled, taken risks, built a real sense of mutual trust in their coleadership capabilities, and had produced together a product—the group plan—that they were ready to put into effect.

And, through it all, they looked forward to working as coleaders. They had recognized that being business partners demanded from them a considerable amount of cooperation, but, at the same time, they functioned independently in their practice. This group coleadership, to do it right, forced them truly to collaborate as they created their group plan together. They were confident that they would now be able to function well together as group leaders and that the postsession debriefing sessions they intended to hold would prove useful to that end. Of course, about all that, only time would tell.

Bill Johnson continually asked himself why he couldn't get himself straightened out. He wondered over and over if the group at the Y would be any good and why he didn't find a high-powered private therapist somewhere, as he suspected most of his colleagues would do. And, running through all of this, Bill debated about whether he would be able to let his defenses down to get the kind of help he knew he needed. Despite much wavering and with these considerable doubts, however, Bill decided to give it a chance, and he enrolled for the pregroup interview.

In truth, and not too deeply below the surface, Bill hoped that what was wrong with him was minor and could be easily fixed. Once done, he would then be returned to his old, familiar self-confidence.

Many new clients feel this way, after all. It's similar to taking a car with bad brakes to the repair shop to get them fixed to function again as they did before. Experts work their magic on the malfunctioning part, repairing it to work well once again. In this mechanistic view, the "malfunctioning part" need do nothing. The expert simply fixes it, restoring it to worthy service.

Well, this was Bill's thinking as he sat down with Fred and Heather for his pregroup interview. Plus, he was aware of his heart beating quickly and some unusually sweaty palms. And his voice—somehow it seemed strangely to quiver at first.

It wasn't all so bad, and Bill began to relax a bit. The group leaders looked over the form that Bill had completed a few moments before and asked him several questions that seemed surprisingly easy to answer. He remembered some of them: What kind of law do you practice? How do you feel about being a lawyer? Any physical problems? Taking any medication regularly? What is bothering you? How about friends, relationships? Those last two were a little more difficult—they got closer to his hurt.

He recalled feeling relief that he was getting through this first hurdle without "breaking," without appearing weak and needy. How long he could maintain what he knew was a facade worried him, yet he knew he must try. Appearing strong and in control of his life—always easy in the past—felt now more like a rule to be followed, even if not genuinely experienced. It was already becoming clear that he valued invulnerability over leveling with others to get the kind of help he really did need.

At the end of the pregroup interview, the group counselors described the new personal growth group for professionals that the Y was offering. Basically, they said that the group was to begin next Thursday night and run for 10 consecutive weeks, with each group session lasting from 7:30 to 9:30 p.m. There would be up to 10 members, professionals of both sexes who were feeling a need to examine and improve their psychological lives, their work, and their relationships. The group would be led by them and it would give lots of opportunity for members to talk about themselves and to give and receive "feedback," or their impressions and observations. As well, the sessions might include some use of structured exercises to help move things along and to focus energies. The first session, next Thursday, would be devoted to meeting one another and learning in more detail about the group and each other. At that point, the counselors stressed (or at any time, for that matter), members could decide to continue or discontinue with the experience.

"From what you have told me," Fred said, "I recommend that you try this group. I think it could be very helpful. What do you think?"

Bill had known most of this about the group through the description he had read. But hearing it directly from the two leaders hit him quite a bit more strongly. Ten sessions at two hours each, that's 20 hours, minimum. And in a group—do I really need a group? And with people I don't even know! I want to get shaped up and on with my life. It's scary. But these thoughts were countered with others: I'm not doing anything with that time anyway, not now. Am I free then? Yes, I guess so. Maybe being with people I don't know would be good. But will I be able to do OK in a group?

Bill asked about that last question, "I know this is a group we are talking about. I don't know, really, if that would be best for me. Is a group a good idea?"

Heather responded. "I think this group is tailor-made for a person with your life experience and concerns. Being with other professionals, all of whom are asking similar questions, guided by experienced group leaders, seems to me to address your needs most directly. The interpersonal support and feedback you could gain would be invaluable to your growth, I think. More so than you could get from individual counseling, for instance. So I do recommend the group for you. What do you say? It's your choice."

Searching for a way to look and sound positive and certain, he said (maybe a little too strongly and impulsively), "OK, sign me up!" But then his reservations, mixed with a testiness that was also real, came through. "I'll see what happens the first time."

Done. Launch time was T – 6 days—and counting!

THE FIRST MEETING

Bill was the first one there, that is, except for Heather and Fred, who warmly introduced themselves to him. He made special note of Heather, whose attractiveness was immediately apparent. But, then, he quickly checked that, telling himself that this certainly was not the time or place for that kind of thing.

His attention shifted. Why am I always on time, no, early, for things? Bill berated himself. It's downright disgusting to be so prompt. Where are the others? Isn't this group going to happen? he continued, while half-hoping it would be canceled.

The answer to his question came quickly as several people began to filter into the room. Silently, with many furtive glances, as if they were testing the waters very carefully, they came.

The group was on after all. Blast off was about to occur. Buckle up, he murmured under his breath, as Heather began to speak.

Heather began to orient the members to the group. Fred, her coleader, observed the members, the setting, the mood. This looks good, he judged. Everybody is here, all eight. We are getting started just about on time, which doesn't always happen in a first session. They may wonder why there is no table between us, why we sit in a small circle. We'll see. I'm anxious, I know that, I always am in these first sessions. Good that Heather and I are sitting opposite each other so we can observe each other and communicate better. She seems relaxed as she is speaking. I'll have to ask her about that later. I think we are getting off to a good start.

And so Heather and Fred introduced themselves and their group-leading qualifications to the members. This was followed by self-introductions by each of the members.

Nothing out of the ordinary here, thought Heather following the go-round. Everyone seems to belong here. All professionals in their midtwenties to midforties, five women and three men, all concerned in some way with their lives, no really bizarre or psychotic stuff, most being pretty protective right now, all just testing the situation—trying to determine if they want to be here or not.

Bill was taking all this in, gauging its value, assessing the level of risk. He was aware that he didn't want to reveal too much yet, or maybe ever, to these perfect strangers. While he was somewhat interested in the members, he was far more focused on the group leaders, Fred and Heather. After all, they were the experts, they were the leaders. Bill was keenly aware of watching them, waiting for them to do something special, wanting them to show the way. And, above all else, he had one very big question: Is this the place for me?

"You are all probably wondering to yourselves how this group is going to be, if it is the right kind of experience for you?" offered Fred. Bill was amazed at how Fred was almost reading his mind.

Fred went on. "Well, this is one of the main purposes of this first session, that is, to help you to learn more about the group and for each of you to determine if you want to continue with it. So, Heather and I would like to tell you something about the purposes of this personal growth group for professionals and about how, in general, we anticipate it may operate."

The coleaders then took turns sharing with the members some of the main aspects of their group plan. They had this information outlined on a one-page handout, which Heather distributed. Essentially, it was an elaboration of the same information that Heather and Fred had provided earlier in the individual interviews. Now, though, the group leaders gave some examples and invited questions.

Sometimes, of course, early in a group members ask precious few questions at this point. The group leader then is faced with working very hard to stimulate involvement. Not so in this case. Questions there were!

"Are we going to sit in a circle like this every time?" "How can we be sure that whatever we say in here is kept among us and doesn't get spread all over the place?" "Are all 10 weeks really necessary or can we get through things faster?" "How were we selected to participate?" "Are these kinds of groups as good as seeing a counselor individually?" "You said we could decide to leave the group, if we thought that necessary. How does that happen?" "What do you mean by structured exercises?" "Will we go for two hours straight or will there be a break?" "I've been in a group something like this before and I remember lots of pushing, lots of pressure from the leader. Is this going to be like that?"

To inexperienced and unprepared group leaders, these kinds of questions can be shocking—totally and completely unnerving. Failing to respond adequately can set the stage for the downfall of the group. Even though Heather and Fred fit neither the category inexperienced nor unprepared, these questions were still quite challenging and sometimes difficult for them to answer well. But they had decided long before in their planning that the best way to handle such matters was to respond directly and fully and not to evade or to be defensive. They had anticipated that this group of high-powered professionals might ask tough questions and that they would expect direct answers, despite whatever psychological problems they were experiencing. They were right.

Bill listened carefully to how the group leaders responded to these questions. He figured that this would tell a whole lot about their abilities and their interest in actually being helpful. It might even determine if he would remain in this group. Actually, they seemed to be very much more willing to respond to some questions than he ever would have been.

Imagine, he thought, if I behaved this way with any of my clients! In the first place, they wouldn't dare ask such questions. I wonder why Heather and Fred are so—I don't know—accepting of all this?

Bill was having a hard time, also, deciding if he liked the way these coleaders were responding. For instance, about the possibility of having a break during the two-hour sessions. The idea that we could all judge that and together make a decision, once we had been involved for a couple of group sessions, was appealing, yet, he thought, kind of wishy-washy. Or, in response to another member's (was it Judy's, he couldn't be sure of the name) fear that the leaders would be pushy, they had offered that this is sometimes an issue for different group members and that, while some may judge the leaders to be that way, others may think them to be not forceful enough. Whatever the case, this was an area to be monitored carefully and considered as the group evolved, they had suggested. Well, he wondered, would they or wouldn't they?

He was getting frustrated about their style, their equivocal way of responding. They didn't give the kind of crisp answers that he was accustomed to in the world of law and business. They didn't seem decisive. There were few black-and-white, yes-no rules here. Couldn't they have said, for instance, Yes, there will be one 15-minute break every session, from 8:30 to 8:45. Or, no, we will never be pushy, we can guarantee it. What gives? he stewed.

A lull fell over the group. It appeared that all questions had been asked and answered, at least for now. But Bill was still working on his frustration, this time debating internally with whether he should bring this whole thing up. Finally, just as Heather began to suggest that they move on, he decided to act.

"Why can't you just give a simple yes or no answer to our questions?" he interrupted. "Everything is so vague, so negotiable. What's the point?"

This was a confrontation, not a question. Fred and Heather were not really prepared for it. Usually, this level of interaction does not occur until later in a group's development. When it does happen early it can be very destructive; if handled well, which is difficult, it can propel a group forward.

But Fred took up the gauntlet, with little pause, and with a calm voice. "I sense very much, Bill, that you want us to be more decisive. To set limits, to kind of lay down specific rules to be followed and enforced. But I wonder if you can appreciate what we are attempting to do right now . . . we are trying to work with all of you to create a group experience that will be *ours*—all of ours—and just not the property of the leaders. This group is not Heather's and mine alone, even though we are its leaders. It is not appropriate for us to set all the rules, to make all the decisions. When we feel there is a time in the future to be decisive and to set limits, then you can be assured that we will do so. I wonder—can you buy into that for now, Bill?"

Maybe it was his way of testing and being contentious, Bill didn't know. Most probably it was a way to help him to decide if this group was for him or not. Perhaps he attacked because it's a style he uses to gain or, more often, to regain, control of a situation. Whatever it was, Bill very much liked the way that Fred had responded to him. He allowed that it took some guts for Fred not to lose his "cool" and to state a clear position. It occurred to Bill that Fred, in fact, had just shown the kind of decisiveness that he was demanding—without deviating from his course. Satisfied, Bill was quick to let Fred know that he thought he could buy into it.

And more than that, although he didn't say so, Bill knew then that he would be continuing with this group.

Chapter 10

LOOKING AT SESSION ONE: DEPENDENCY

HEATHER AND FRED MEET FOR POSTSESSION PROCESSING

When coleaders meet to analyze their work in a group session, they call it "processing." It means going over and over what happened, why it may have happened, how various group members seem to be doing, and—very important—how each group leader is doing and feeling. All this is done to be sure that the group service is being delivered in the best possible way, that individual members are being given sufficient opportunity to grow and change, and that the leaders are functioning as effectively as possible toward these ends.

This coleader processing provides qualified professionals with an ongoing, mutual supervision experience. It is one of the several reasons that many group counseling theorists prefer a coleadership situation over a solo one, where no built-in supervisory opportunity is possible.

This processing can get very intense. Leaders who are committed to learning from each other are the most able to engage fully. Using the norms of everyday life as a guide, the conversations these kinds of coleaders sometimes engage in—when they are giving each other feedback, for instance—might be labeled as "brutally frank," or "very impolite." Conversely, other conversations, in which leaders may express some very warm feelings of support, or cry from deep pangs of regret for something untimely they may have said to a group member, might be tagged as being "too close," or as "so weak." In truth, these sorts of interactions are often the most fruitful for spurring on the enhancement or refinement of group leader skills.

Now, not all of these discussions are high voltage in nature. But, when things are going well, their level of intensity is typically quite high. For it

70

is through the open exchange of information and the mutual sharing of honest feeling that coleaders can best learn from each other and be able to advance their practice. If the leaders are reluctant to take risks with each other, if they choose to be self-protective, the level of processing can be quite matter of fact, almost as if the coleaders were holding a detached assessment of an uneventful play. And the resulting benefits of this form of controlled processing are almost always diminished. All of this comes close to a maxim, of sorts: high risk, high gain; and its corollary: low risk, low gain.

Heather and Fred were just about to begin their first processing session. As might be expected, they had discussed postsession processing during their planning meetings. They were aware that some coleaders prefer to meet immediately following a group session, because then everything is fresh. Leaders subscribing to this viewpoint think that meeting right afterward would give them the fullest access to the most accurate data about the session, and that they are then on a kind of "roll," being best able to interact energetically and genuinely with each other. But Heather and Fred also knew that other coleaders choose to allow some amount of time to pass before holding a processing meeting. Group leaders holding this position think that there is much merit in allowing the heat of the moment to dissipate, that some amount of objectivity is useful for valid and reliable processing, and that recharging their batteries for processing leads to a higher-quality, more focused effort.

Fred and Heather had decided on a kind of compromise, although favoring the latter course. They agreed to meet on Friday afternoons from 1:00 to 3:00. Doing so would give a break of several hours from the previous Thursday night group session, including a night's sleep. They had discussed meeting on Monday or Tuesday, but dismissed that due to the intervening weekend, which they both thought would provide too much of a break. They had also agreed to write individual notes as soon after each group session as possible in an effort to retain the most important group events and their reaction to them. They felt confident that these notes would prove to be very useful in their processing the next day.

And so they met in Heather's office this time, to reflect on the first session and to determine if their plan for session two still made sense, given the occurrences of session one. They both were aware of being eager, yet anxious, about their meeting as they sat down to begin.

"You know, Fred," volunteered Heather, "I'm about as antsy right now as I was last night at 7:30, just before the session! Well, maybe not quite, but I do confess to a lot of anxiety. I'm not really sure why."

"It's the same for me," Fred said. "I think it has to do with beginning something important and not knowing how it's going to go."

"Somehow admitting this right up front seems helpful," disclosed Heather. "I'm beginning to feel a little less tense. And, anyway, we have a good base to be working from, what with the hours of planning. Why don't we get started, Fred?"

"Actually, I thought we were doing it already. We have to start somewhere and talking about how we are feeling now is as legitimate as anything else, wouldn't you say?"

"OK, of course," said Heather, hurriedly. "Yes, Fred, but I mean to get started in looking at last night's session. I'm really curious. Can I ask—what did you make of it?"

"OK," said Fred. "Let me first quickly look at the notes I jotted down last night about the session." Heather took this time to look at her notes, too.

In Fred's view, the session went well. "I was pleased that everyone showed up and was on time. I guess that's the first test for me. At the end, as I think of all the members, it appears that they have all determined to return for more. They seemed to tie into the group pretty well. And that's the second test at this stage of a group."

"And what's the third test? Everything comes in three's, right?" asked Heather.

"I don't know, maybe. All right, probably the third test would be how I felt through all this. And I felt about the right amount of energy and pins and needles, although toward the end, I must say, Bill did kind of throw me for a loop!"

"I'll say," agreed Heather. "But I was so impressed by how you handled that! And, frankly, I'm real glad you did pick up on that because I was blown away by it. For me, the whole session was basically predictable and going well until that point."

"Yeah, who would have expected such a burst of fire so early? You thought I did OK with that?" asked Fred, wanting to be sure of Heather's evaluation.

"I thought about it a lot last night," Heather continued. "And I just couldn't imagine handling that whole thing any better than you did. I'm afraid I would have stammered a whole lot, or just sat in a cold sweat not knowing what to do."

"Thanks. I just decided to plunge in and see what would happen. Once I got started I was OK, I sort of knew what I wanted to say. And it worked out—at least this time! But we will need to watch for Bill, I think. Of all the members, he seems to have a lot of steam building below that pleasant surface. It looks like something is really boiling away in there and, if the end of our first session is any sample of things to come, I'll bet this isn't the last we'll see. But I don't want to overinterpret at this point, either. How about if we pick up on this whole thing a little later?

"I did want to ask you something, Heather. Right at the beginning of the session, when you were leading the introductions, I was feeling pretty anxious. You said today that you were, too. But I remember observing you then and you seemed so absolutely cool, in control. How were you feeling?"

Heather remembered very well. She was like a cat on a hot tin roof. But she had learned in her training to relax enough to be able to adequately control such anxiety, to manage it. And going first, having some kind of structure even to use, was usually very successful for her in doing so.

"I could have jumped right out of my skin. I'll never stop feeling that kind of performer's anxiety, or whatever it is. Starting off is often helpful to me in managing it. If I sit for long without participating, it becomes much worse. In fact, that could be something for me to work on a little during this group, if possible. But I am very interested in getting your impressions of how I came across then. It's a relief that I seemed to be acting naturally because I think that's what group members need to see in their leaders, especially at the beginning, and that is certainly how I want to be seen. Does that make sense to you, Fred?"

"Perfect sense. And, as I say, you really did seem to be natural and in control, which probably helped members to feel that the group might be a safe place to be."

"Could we go back to Bill? Do you think there was anything about what he accused us of—indecisiveness was his theme, as I recall—that rings true?"

Heather had wondered about that, too. She knew very well that group leaders often find themselves as targets at some point in the group just because they are the designated leaders. At the same time, this was the very first session, a time when most members tend to show a real sense of dependency on them. It was a bit out of synch she thought, which is why she was so affected by Bill's confrontation. Could that mean that Bill was picking up on a real deficit in their group leading styles, she had asked herself? Or is Bill acting out, again rather early, some very ineffective behavior that has gotten him into trouble elsewhere? And— that may be a way that Bill shows his dependence?"

"I must confess to being unsure right now," said Heather, quickly adding, "And I can hear Bill roaring immediately about indecisiveness! We are trying to establish norms together as a group, which requires us to refrain from calling the shots, after all. No, I think we were OK, doing well, in fact. But I do agree with what you suggested earlier, Fred. I think we will need to be especially sensitive to Bill in the future—and I think we will need to make it a point to monitor our own level of participation with regard to the decisiveness issue."

"I'm relieved to hear you say that, Heather," he paused. "You know, as I remember it, absolutely no one else chimed in with Bill about this decisiveness issue, leading me to think it may be more idiosyncratic to him. And yet, because dependence ought to be the order of the day at a group's start, maybe expecting a chorus of shouting behind Bill then would be unrealistic, anyway. Yeah, it's my best guess that this may be more Bill's issue and not our's, and definitely not the group's. And, unless I may be way off base here, I think it very likely that attacking may be how he deals with dependence. You know, the best defense is a good offense, or something like that. Now, if all that is accurate, I am thinking that our plan for next session still holds. How about you?"

"Yes, even more so, perhaps. Providing more structure will help to focus members on their goals, plus help us to move things along a little more quickly. Only having 10 weeks is not much time. And—I just thought of two more reasons," she laughed. "I've told you that some structuring helps me feel more comfortable and, I should think, now that we know him a little bit, Bill, too!"

BILL REFLECTS ON THE FIRST SESSION

Bill was wound up right after the session. It was at times like these—and they had been coming much more frequently in the last few months—that he longed for a good friend to talk to, someone he could bounce his thoughts off of. That there really was no one was one of the banes of his existence.

So, he found himself heading for the Moonbeam, an upscale bar that was currently in considerable favor among the Yuppie crowd on his side of town. Though he could certainly not be considered a regular there, it was a place Bill liked. Its variety of settings allowed for mingling with others or watching sports on the big-screen TV, sitting quietly with a companion, or finding your own niche for some private time (as private as it gets in a place like that) just to think.

Actually, he realized, as he pulled once again into the overflowing parking lot—but this time to get lucky and find a spot—this was the first time he had been out in the evening for weeks. Why now? Was the group already having some kind of magic effect? he wondered with an inner grin.

Miraculously, his favorite solo table was free, the one in the corner of the chess room, overlooking the lake. (Maybe his fortune was on the upswing, after all!) He took it, looked out the window to see the moon glimmering on the water on this clear night and the sailboats all moored in neat little rows. All a most comforting sight, and something he felt he needed, especially right now.

He ordered a beer and turned his thoughts to the group he had just left. What in the world was that all about, he wondered? He had a lot of loose ends, anathema to him, that he needed to tie up.

He hated having mixed feelings and a buzzing confusion in his head! But that was truly his state now and the group session had only added to it. The session had been good, bad, scary, boring, all of these, and more.

He was aware that his predominate feelings were anchored on the leaders, Heather and Fred. There was no question that Heather was very cute, and he loved her smile. But he also knew, as he had warned himself earlier, that this was something he had to put out of his mind. Besides, she was probably married or maybe even involved with Fred, who knows? Aside from all that, Heather had kept things moving, helped everyone to get acquainted, and he liked that. With regard to her counterpart, thought Bill, Fred seemed awfully laid back, except toward the end when he came on like "gangbusters." He was more of an enigma.

What bothered Bill the most was this whole business of the leaders leading. In fact, he was still reeling some from being so riled up about it in the group that he had stuck his neck out, challenging Heather and Fred. But maybe they were leading just the right amount for this kind of group; maybe he was expecting something there that was not appropriate?

With regard to jumping on Heather and Fred, he felt both justified— as if he were leading the charge for the group—and embarrassed, too. Was I speaking for the others, he wondered? And this whole thing about jumping on others; I seem to be doing that more and more . . .

I have no idea how others in my life view me now, in fact, I never have, he worried. Once proud of that fact, it now upset him a great deal. I wonder how Heather and Fred see me? How the other members do? (What are their names? I can't remember one of them except, maybe, for Judy.)

It's a strange experience, all right, that group. I feel kind of naked in there, and like a babe in the woods, unprotected, never knowing what's going to happen next, and what's going to be required of me. I want the leaders to help out with all that, damn it, to lead the way!

All in all, Bill decided again, as he stood to leave, there is something about that group that pushes me, that attracts me. I know a big part of it was what Fred said toward the end. I'd like to see more of that kind of thing.

But, it feels like there must be more to it, other things that are drawing me. What?

He turned this over in his mind as he made his way out of the Moonbeam to his car, oblivious of the crowd and the hustling going on in the bar area. What was that tune he had begun to hum, the one that had been playing in the Moonbeam as he walked out? Yes, that's it, he suddenly recalled, the old James Taylor song (or was it Carol King's?), "You've Got a Friend."

So reassuring, thought Bill. And then, quickly, he wondered if it was that very message that was tugging at him from the group . . . there were others there who, in some ways, seemed a whole lot like him. The one guy, Peter, was it, who is a CPA and says he's been feeling lost lately, unsure of who he is and what he really wants out of life. That seemed, oh, so familiar. Somehow, knowing that another person is in the same boat was comforting. How bizarre, he thought.

I don't know, maybe there's something there, Bill reflected, as he pulled away, headed for home. It's worth going back to see.

Chapter 11

REAL CONFLICT IN THE GROUP

Sessions two and three of the group had come and gone, evidenced by a growing closeness and a warm sense of safety. In session two, Heather and Fred had helped the members to arrive at a workable understanding of confidentiality: Basically, that members were free to discuss their own material outside the group but nothing about anybody else, except in only the most general way. The group also had come to a shared conception of some other important rules and norms. Perhaps the one norm that took the longest to clarify had to do with distinguishing between attacking and confronting. This one was all tied up with concerns about feeling safe in the group. Attacking was ruled out, while "constructive" confrontation was endorsed.

Then, in session three, a structured exercise had been introduced by the coleaders, called "Life-line." In this exercise, each person was to graph the high- and the low-points of their lives according to five-year intervals. These graphs were then shown to the others and explained. Each member was to take 10 to 15 minutes for their "turn." The purpose of this exercise was to provide a safe opportunity for self-disclosure.

This Life-line exercise seemed to work extremely well. In fact, it proved so difficult to contain the individual sharing within the time frame allotted that Fred and Heather allowed the proceedings to go past the agreed-upon two hours by 25 minutes. It all seemed worthwhile, though, as the quality of involvement appeared to be high.

And so the fourth session of the group was about to begin, emerging from these two positive and productive sessions. Fred and Heather were aware that one-third of the group's life was now over and they were preparing to help the members to begin working on their personal growth in earnest. They were looking forward to a very productive

session, with a focus on the identification of personal goals for the group
and how these could be reached. They had decided, also, that the need
for structure was beginning to subside in the group. In their best
estimate, the members were now ready to take greater responsibility for
moving and shaping group interaction.

They were in for a surprise.

Heather began the session, after waiting for eight minutes for the late
arrival of Bill.

"Well, now that we are all here, let's try to build from the good work of
last session by becoming more focused on what it is that each of you
really wants to accomplish in this group. We now know a bit about some
of the important events of each other's lives. But the question is now,
what do each of you need to do to progress further personally and
professionally? And—most important—how can this group be helpful
in that regard?"

"We have no structured exercise prepared for this, as we did last week
and the week before," added Fred. "That might only get in the way now.
We think the group is ready to move very well right now without an
exercise to help it."

After a short pause, Heather asked, encouragingly, "All right, can we
begin?"

You could have heard a pin drop.

The truth be known, Bill had been seething since the last session. He
did not much appreciate what he viewed as the "wastefulness" of last
week. Spending all of that time talking about the past, about history that
was long gone. Life-line! It was time to change some *lives* (as for his own,
he wasn't convinced), not to wallow in lifelines. In fact, he wasn't at all
sure that he was that interested in knowing about these people's pasts,
what happened to them at age five, for Pete's sake! Who cares? Why is
that useful? What can be done about that now? And, furthermore, he
was certain he did not want to tell them about anything really significant
about his past; nothing, for instance, about Chelsea and her death. So he
had played a game, kept things under control, telling just enough to go
along with things but not enough to expose himself.

But much more distressing to Bill than all that had been the time spent
going way beyond the 9:30 closing hour. He had realized being bothered
about it some at the time. As the week went on, though, he grew angrier.
To him, his time was very valuable. He didn't squander it (in fact, the
billable minutes of his law practice had ground it into him to always use
time to its maximum advantage), and he certainly could not allow others
to waste it for him!

And so Bill showed up late for the session. Not incredibly late, mind you, not late so-as-to-obviously-state-a-message. But, pleasingly (to him) late. Sort of "getting back" just a little, regaining some of his lost time. Taking back some of the control.

He didn't know, or care very much, what the other members were feeling as Heather and Bill introduced this fourth session. He did see quite clearly that no one was exactly jumping at the opportunity to state their personal and professional goals, or whatever they were being asked to do. He also realized—quite consciously—that he was not going to participate for a while. It was a kind of protest, a holding out. The leaders think everything is so great here, let them deal with it, let *them* work it out!

In their own ways, each of the group members was choosing to be noninvolved. This set of choices produces a blockage resulting, at least for now, in a thundering silence.

Judy broke the silence, to just about everyone's relief.

"I didn't get a chance last week to tell you about what I think was the very important role my older brother, Tom, played in my life. I don't know, we just didn't seem to have time. But he was such an achiever, so absolutely excellent at everything he did, that I think I was left somewhere in the dust. At least that's what my therapist has said in the past."

Peter immediately picked up with this theme of being left behind by talking about his father, who, when Peter was in Junior High School, divorced Peter's mother. Peter reported a feeling of being ignored and maybe even abandoned after that by his dad.

Then there was another silence. Bill was stewing. Here we go, again, he thought. What's happening here? The leaders ask for one thing to be done, no one does it. Instead, some people start to tell stories again. Then no one speaks, once more. This is one huge waste of my time. And Bill could resist no longer.

"This is crazy!" Bill blurted out. "What is it that is going on here? I don't know about you, but *I* certainly do not have the time for this! And you (he said, pointing to the leaders) just sit there and allow this nonsense to continue. I have just about had it with this whole idea!"

Heather responded, after a moment to catch her composure.

"Bill, I very much hear your frustration at how things are going tonight so far and at what Fred and I are doing, too. I think this is something we need to look at directly—and right now," said Heather.

She went on. "How are the rest of you feeling about tonight's session? It's really important for us to get our impressions out on the table. It's only then that we can do something constructive about what is happening."

This question of Heather's seemed to take the lid off of a boiling pot. As contrasted with the long silences earlier in the session, several group members were able to offer their observations and to express their feelings. Not all of this was on the strongly negative end, as was Bill's. Some, such as Judy, were enjoying the opportunity to get to know one another better and to learn about some of the context of people's lives. Judy said she liked it when the leaders let them talk, allowed some freer time to learn about each other. She had found this interesting and beneficial and, in fact, would like to continue it. Others, such as Peter, were unsure about moving on and what he would be asked to do. It was more comfortable for him to talk about things that had already happened than to open himself up to the future and how he could change it, even though this was really why he was here. Bill, of course, was clear that he was uninterested in all the "historical stuff," as he put it, and he was very angry about going way overtime last week.

Judy asked Bill why he had not said any of this last week, instead of waiting until now, when it was wrapped up in all his anger?

And—all of a sudden—both Heather and Fred recognized that the group was entering into a new realm of interaction. This emergence was toward the present and away from the past.

Bill struggled with responding directly and honestly, and decided to do so.

"I don't know, Judy," began Bill. "I guess maybe I was afraid then to rock the boat. I have been doing a lot of that lately and I'm not sure it's a good thing for me to be doing. So I held off."

"I, for one, am interested in what you think, in how you are feeling," invited Judy.

"And, what's more, Bill, it seems to me that maybe you have opened up for the group something that's very important," broke in Fred. "I mean it seemed to me that something was in the way of our moving on to goals. Remember the silences? Maybe by voicing your discontent you allowed us all to bring out what it was that we were feeling that was getting in the way. Or that we needed to attend to. I want you to know, Bill, that you have performed a kind of service for the group, in my mind. We need to explore and try to work through our conflicts, just as much as we need to applaud our successes."

"Well, that's all well and good," said Bill. "But where do we go from here?"

Heather spoke. "First, I wonder if you heard the support from both Judy and Fred, Bill?"

Bill had not let it sink in. He admitted to being too busy being angry.

"Second," Heather went on, "the question you raise of where we go from here is an excellent one. It's the question I think we need to ask as a group and to decide as a group, too. Where do we go from here?"

And the group members discussed where to go from here. With the leaders' help, they began to see that they were at a kind of transition point, moving from looking at the past toward envisioning their future, both as a group and for each of them as individuals. They began to see how their uncertainty with this transition may have resulted in the conflict with which they had been just dealing.

Finally, toward the end of the session, as a collective they decided next week to pick up with where the leaders had begun this session: identifying their personal and professional goals for this group. They left energized.

Chapter 12

EXAMINING THE SESSION OF CONFLICT

HEATHER AND FRED MEET

Sometimes when coleaders get together to process the previous group sessions they, too, can experience delays, blocks, or other sorts of diversions in their interaction. In this sense, the group coleader relationship is subject to the same dynamics as is the group they are leading. This processing session was a case in point for Heather and Fred, at least at the beginning.

"Whew, has today been hectic!" began Fred.

"For you, too?" asked Heather. "It seems that the last three weeks or so have been just unbelievable for me. And the upcoming convention adds just one more big responsibility. Which reminds me—we haven't even begun to write our paper."

"I know," offered Fred quite sheepishly, as he was to have produced a first draft by last week. "I just haven't been able to get at it, given everything else."

And so it went for another 10 minutes. Heather and Fred, gathered together to process their ongoing group, talked about other matters of concern to them. But not about the last group session. And time, precious time, was elapsing all too quickly.

It is entirely possible, but not responsible to their goal, that an entire processing session could continue in this vein. When such an event occurs, it is most likely that the coleaders are avoiding their work. It would be preferable in such situations for coleaders to create extra time where they can discuss other extragroup matters that need to be examined. It is critical that they be able to regulate their interaction so that their primary purpose—monitoring the group and their leadership of it—is addressed directly. All of this points to the importance of coleaders attending to the quality of their own working relationship and executing a commitment to keeping themselves on task.

"You know, Fred," said Heather, "it just strikes me that we might be guilty of doing what was going on in our group last session—I'm wondering if we are not ready to get down to work about the group? Are we avoiding? Is there some kind of conflict underneath here somewhere? I know I'm feeling like I'm running away a bit, kind of skirting the group. And I'm feeling that it's time I stopped doing that."

It takes one of the pair to identify the blocked responsibly or at least to call the question. At any rate, it involves taking the risk with your partner in an attempt to correct the flow of discussion and to get the coleader processing back on track. That is what Heather was trying to do.

And so they were able to take a look at what was occurring between them at that point. Doing so requires the second person, in this case Fred, to be nondefensive and open to here-and-now examination of their working relationship. Even with group coleaders, this ideal condition may not be sufficiently present. Fortunately, Fred and Heather did enjoy this kind of working relationship.

"I'm glad you brought this up, Heather. And you're right, I think. We're drifting away from why we're here. For some reason, I needed to do that for a while today. Maybe we both did? I know there's a lot on my mind, a lot to do, maybe I just needed to let off some of that. Perhaps we should purposefully set aside some time so we can do that? But at the same time I have been probably resisting getting to work here. But let's get to work!"

With that behind them, the coleaders began to examine the last group session and they were able to do so with renewed clarity and energy.

"So, to the group, what about the group?" asked Heather aloud, almost rhetorically, while she sought to recall clearly what had happened.

Fred rushed in. "I remember one overwhelming reaction I had to what happened last time. A mild case of shock. Yes, that's it. I was really stunned when all we got was a yawning cavern of silence early on! And then as things went on I think I began to understand what was happening. The members helped a lot with that, and so did you, Heather. *They* weren't ready to go on for any number of reasons, while *we* were. So the group had hit a logjam. I don't know, but that's kind of how I see it . . ."

"Yeah, I agree, and the logjam, as you call it, Fred, was really a conflict, right? I think we agreed about that in the session itself. I mean the fact that different members were not ready to move on while we were encouraging them to do so put us at opposing places. But it was all so subtle. It took me quite a while to identify it. But, now that I have, it makes perfectly good sense. I mean developmentally. It was probably time that some kind of conflict emerged in the group. We were ready for it, don't you think, Fred?"

"Are you suggesting that all that group developmental theory you learn in group counseling classes actually makes practical sense?" laughed Fred.

"Yeah, I guess you're right," he continued, becoming serious once again. "That's helpful to put it into the context of theory. And that's what we were getting at, too, toward the end of the session when we talked about 'transition.' Now that some actual conflict has emerged and we have all confronted it and come through it, maybe we are making a transition into a more productive working stage of the group, one where a real cohesion will be present. What do you think?"

"I think that's a real textbook explanation," she laughed, getting back at Fred for his earlier facetiousness. "And I think it probably rings true. At least I hope so. I would look forward to that. Not that conflict is over and done with, or that we might now never expect to hit any more difficulties. But maybe we are a more mature group developmentally, more adept at handling disagreeable situations."

"And we will have some of those," offered Fred as he picked up on Heather's thought.

"I'm thinking of Bill right now," Fred continued. "I 'stroked' him last session for his positive contribution to surfacing the group conflict we've been talking about. Remember?"

Heather shook her head affirmatively.

"And that was real. He did really help out. But no one, except for Judy—who was very brave and helped to really turn the group to a here-and-now focus last session—has touched on Bill's hostility and withholding side. I mean, that's the way I'm seeing it. Heather, I see this as something to look out for, maybe even to go after directly. How about you?"

Heather had been thinking about this, too.

"Absolutely, Fred! You remember—how could you forget—how Bill 'attacked' us last week? I'm not at all sure, but I think that was a critical incident. As I recall, I responded to that; sometimes all this gets a bit hazy. But I remember trying to get behind Bill's energy and open his issues about us for the whole group to explore. I wanted to legitimize the conflict and support a group discussion of it. It worked, I think."

"No question about it, Heather. I thought what you did was right on target."

"But at the same time," Heather continued, "what was not done—I think wisely then—was to address Bill directly. I see lots of hostility in him, too. He kind of recoils and boils and then it steams out. Also, do you remember that he came late to the session; we waited for him? And no one picked up on that, either. I'm thinking, though, that if we are evolving as a group, we may be getting enough solidity that we can begin to tackle such threatening stuff, such as Bill's hostility. What do you think about that?"

Fred agreed. "I think it has been important to surface the conflict and to help the group to see it and to deal with it before getting into risky individual-level stuff. My guess is that would have been premature and could have blown the group apart. Yes, I think we are getting ready for this. One of the things to watch out for, for instance, with Bill, is the kind of goals he develops for himself; whether he presents any kind of vulnerability at all, if he himself identifies anything about hostility that he would like to work on in the group. If he does, that would offer an entrée."

"OK, that makes sense," said Heather. "Another thought, with regard to Bill, is that Judy seems to have connected with him. She leveled with him last week and he responded to her, you know, about why he hadn't said anything before about his anger. Doesn't it make sense to look for ways to encourage this kind of interaction between them in the future?"

As Heather and Fred processed the previous session and looked toward the next one, Bill had his own thoughts.

BILL'S THOUGHTS

Back at the Moonbeam, in his favorite spot, Bill considered what had happened at the last group session.

He didn't know whether to feel like a hero or a chicken. About that he acknowledged confusion. He was also beginning to feel drawn into the group, aware of thinking about it more frequently and more positively. All of this was running through his mind. But the image of the "hero" or the "chicken" stuck. What was all that about, he wondered?

As he ran this through and through, over and over, Bill suddenly realized that this—just doing this kind of self-examination—was a totally new experience for him! He didn't really know where it was going, which was troubling to a person who needs answers and control. Yet there seemed to be something almost exhilarating about it all. He had to admit that a kind of awakening seemed to be happening within himself, a sense of self-discovery. With that awareness, he quickly ordered a second beer.

But where was it headed? There it was again, this obsession with outcomes, with control. Maybe, he thought, he needed to break through that preoccupation, maybe it was doing him little good. Why not let things happen more freely, the Beatles's "Let it be?" Sounds good, maybe even necessary for him, but maybe this is where the chicken comes in.

Am I afraid to let go, he wondered? Am I afraid to turn over control to others, such as to Judy, who got me to go further than I wanted last time?

But the hero in him, the guy who takes on authority aggressively, the guy who "takes the bull by the horns," the guy who controls situations and produces answers, might not let that happen.

All this rumination was leading Bill to sense a conflict that seemed to exist within himself. He was caught in an internal struggle between the "strong" hero and what he saw as the "chicken," not an attractive label at all.

Is that part of the problem, he wondered? Do I equate giving up control and becoming more vulnerable with being a chicken? And does that negative association, at least in part, keep me from moving more in that direction?

He didn't know, and he simply hated that state of not knowing. But, he allowed, maybe this was something that kept him locked, too. Having to have the answers all worked out, to be on top. To not waste time exploring . . .

Could he change? Should he change? What would the next session bring?

With a start, Bill decided to stop all this self-examination for now. The NCAAs were on the big screen in the next room. Better check it out, he could take this only so far right now.

Chapter 13

COHESION BEGINS TO EMERGE AROUND BILL

It doesn't always work this way. But the energy and clarity of purpose that was present toward the end of session four was markedly evident at the start of session five. To begin with, every one was on time. Heather noted that.

"Well, we are all here—and at the absolute stroke of 7:30, too!" she observed. Heather then asked, "I wonder what that means?"

Very quickly, Peter responded.

"For the first time, really, I want to be here tonight," began Peter. "I felt very good as I left last time, especially with what happened at the end. I'm not exactly sure where we are headed, of course, but I do think we are headed in an exciting direction . . . I want to be able to work on personal goals here."

Others reinforced Peter's perception. Even Bill, who said, "Yeah, I'm wanting to 'get on with the show.' Let's get some focus here on what people want to get out of this whole thing."

Heather, who was somewhat partial to using structured exercises in groups, flashed on one that she thought might be particularly useful for focusing the members on personal goals. In it, members are asked to identify and list up to three goals that are important to them and which they think they could work on in the group. The members are then asked to pick a partner from the group and to spend 45 minutes sharing and receiving feedback about their possible goals. At the end of this discussion, each partner is asked to choose the main goal he or she wants to pursue in the group. When the partners are invited back into the large group, each member is asked to share the chosen goal, and to describe a bit of the process that occurred in its selection. Once that is done, the

leaders and members work with each member to help transform the goal
into a specific and concrete statement, using the "SPAMO" acronym ("Specific, Performance-based, Attainable, Measurable, and
Observable").

The clinker here was that she and Fred had not discussed this
possibility, nor had they planned to use any structured exercise in this
session. At the same time, Heather had a strong intuition that this
exercise could "catch the wave" of excitement and energy that seemed to
be present in the members and help to focus it. She faced a conundrum,
caught between the possibility of a structured exercise that might work
very well and the reality that she and her coleader had not discussed its
use. She decided to go with her intuition, which can be risky business.

Heather addressed Fred directly, with the group members listening to
the coleader conversation.

"Fred, it really seems to me that everyone is ready to go right now with
exploring their personal goals for the group. This is great. And I have an
idea about how to proceed, which I think will be very helpful."

Turning to speak to the group members, Heather explained that she
and Fred generally discuss and agree upon what they plan for each
session. Her idea was new, something that the two of them had not
considered. And she wanted to check it out with Fred to see if he would
validate its use. Or not.

Heather picked up with Fred.

"Can I quickly explain it to you?" she asked him.

"Yes, I'm interested in it, and I appreciate your checking with me on
it," Fred immediately responded.

Relieved, Heather sketched out the idea. Fred liked it, said so, and
then he went on.

"While I do think this exercise could be very useful for us, Heather,
let's check it out with the group to see."

Turning to the members, Fred then asked, "What do you think?"

Of course, this whole process involves considerable venturing. The
coleaders are "sticking their necks out," subjecting not only their idea,
but also their authority, to member rejection. Simultaneously, though,
the coleaders are modeling important attitudes and behaviors for the
members to observe. Not the least of these are respect and open
communication.

The members responded supportively. Judy's summary seemed to
capture the essence of it all.

Judy said, "I trust what you are doing. If you both think this activity
might work, I say—and I think all of us are saying, in one way or

another—let's try it. What's more, I am touched by your effort to talk this over with each other and with us. I think that's wonderful!"

And so the personal goals exercise was conducted. It was interesting that Bill and Judy constituted one of the exercise dyads.

Even more than getting help in focusing his personal goals, working with Judy for those few minutes helped Bill to gain sufficient support and encouragement to identify goals that were real, that actually meant something to him.

He could have done his usual self-protective number. He could have simply thrown out something that seemed on the surface to be genuine but that he really had worked out already. But Judy somehow inspired him to do more. She enabled him to talk about some of his recent concerns about where he was headed with his life. Judy, mostly by listening to him and encouraging him, had been able in a few minutes to help Bill to discuss what it was that he needed to do. And so he did, he got pretty close, and he was prepared to disclose a general goal to the group when it came his turn to do so.

Bill's turn came early. Somehow he came across differently than ever before. A lot of the rough edge was removed, the sharpness. He appeared to be stretching himself now, maybe even opening himself up to the others—and to himself.

Although he had planned on being concise, once he began to identify his personal goal to the group, Bill's words and energy began to build. He was on to something authentic.

Bill began. "I don't know, really, but ever since our last session I have been acting weird. I usually don't spend lots of time wondering about myself and where I'm going. I've prided myself on going out and *doing*, in succeeding. I've been feeling a little lost, though, lately and somehow I have been struggling. I'm not so sure of myself any more. It hurts me to admit that, as you can probably tell by my shaky voice right now . . .

"And there is this something inside my head that I've kind of discovered since last week," Bill went on. "It takes the form of—this may sound strange to all of you—seeing myself as a 'hero' or as a 'chicken.' I have always gloried in being on top of situations, in being the guy who challenges and takes control. On being a 'winner.' A hero. And I am beginning to realize that I may be deathly afraid of showing any weakness at all. I mean, admitting to having difficulties or problems, asking for help, being here; this kind of thing, for me, I see as chicken . . . I don't know where any of this is leading, actually . . . .."

With that, Bill stopped, apparently unable to go on.

Judy, his partner in the exercise, stepped in.

"I really respect your struggling with all this, Bill. I don't know where you want to wind up with it, or how far you want to go right now. Would it help to try to share the main goal that you came up with in our discussion?" Judy asked.

This gentle nudge was all that Bill needed to continue.

"Maybe I can do that. Let's see, I want to get my life on some kind of a better track, to feel more useful in a larger sense, to get more meaning out of what I'm doing. I've been on the fast track to success as a hot-shot lawyer, have found a lot of it, but now at age 30 I suddenly feel kind of empty. No, make that *very* empty! I want a fuller existence, with friends, a real relationship with somebody I can care about, like one I used to have," he shared, his voice trailing off.

Fred responded caringly with feedback. "OK, you've shared a whole lot of personal things, Bill. That takes a lot of courage, especially for someone who—as you described yourself—wants very much to appear in control. I get a real sense that you are moving rapidly right now, working on some concerns that are very important to you. In some ways, it sounds like this kind of personal searching is new for you and you feel vulnerable about it. Also, though, I sense that you are willing to risk this, at least to some extent, because you are motivated enough to change in the direction of becoming better balanced—I'm thinking of the hero and the chicken metaphors you used. Laying out your goals like this, in such a personal way, is the first step in getting assistance through the group, I think. I'm really pleased you have been able to take this step."

Bill found it important to receive this kind of understanding and support from Fred, one of the coleaders. Bill's challenging mode was in abeyance. He wanted, in fact, yearned right now, for acceptance. And he got it.

Heather picked up, offering her support, too. She then said to Bill, "It's important for us to figure out how our group can be helpful to you in reaching your goal. Let's start with you, Bill. What are your thoughts about that?"

Bill knew, at least he had what he thought was a very good idea about this. But he was not at all sure he wanted to bring his thought to light, as it was scary. While he struggled with this ambivalence, a short silence fell upon the group, although it felt like forever to Bill.

Summoning up his courage, Bill replied. "I think I know what I need, but who knows if I can handle it? What I need, I think, is for all of you to be honest with me. For you to tell me what you think of me. For you to give me feedback. That's one frightening proposition. I think the other thing I need to do is to back off my hard-driving, hero stuff. I need to learn other ways to be and not to view them as being a chicken, either. Whew, there I've said it!" ended Bill with a sense of great relief.

Heather responded. "Your goal, to fill out your life, to become better balanced, seems very appropriate, Bill. What I take from what you've said, too, is that a main way that our group can be helpful to you is to give you feedback. You are asking us to tell you how you come across. And, conversely, you are wanting to experiment some, it sounds, with being less in control. I'm not quite sure what that might mean yet in terms of your behavior, but this is what I am hearing from you. Am I getting the right picture, that you are both asking for feedback and wanting to try out new behaviors?" she inquired of Bill.

"Yes, I think so," said Bill. "That's what I'm saying all right. And as I hear it from you, this doesn't at all sound like me, does it?"

Heather replied, quickly. "It sounds to me like a very healthy part of you who is breaking through perhaps an old facade and saying, 'hey, look at me, attend to me; I want to grow and improve.' Wow, I find all that so very encouraging and stimulating. Let's see if we can help support your working on all that."

"Now can we kind of hold it there for a while, Bill?" asked Fred. "We need to try to get around to every one here tonight to identify goals. Keep that energy, though, so we can get back to it."

"Yes, that's fine," said Bill.

And they moved on to complete the goal exercise with the remaining members. The next sessions should be incredible, thought Bill, as this one pulled to a close. Will I be ready?

Chapter 14

PROCESSING THE COHESION STAGE

THE LEADERS CONFER

"That was one of the most productive group sessions I've ever been involved with!" exclaimed the usually restrained Fred, as he and Heather began their coleader processing meeting. "There was such a good flow to it, so much good work. There was no sense of having to dig for things. It seemed that people were 'ready to go,' as I think you put it early in the session."

Heather agreed. "It was fabulous! I really enjoyed being part of that whole thing. All we had to do, it seemed to me, was to provide some stimulus, a little guiding, and they were off and running in positive directions. It was all very rewarding."

Group leading can sometimes be a glorious activity. It is not filled always with struggle, intensity, and conflict. Fred and Heather were able to experience one of these special sessions when the conditions were right for group members to progress swiftly and, seemingly, effortlessly.

Of course, the leaders had had a hand in shaping the conditions of the group up to that point. The group had been evolving, through the dependency and conflict of earlier sessions, to the point of *cohesion*. In this stage, members enter into a period of trust that is real. This trust emerges from the successful resolution of struggle that results in shared understandings of the group's purposes and methods for operation. This laboring involves members grappling with how they fit into the group, what behavior is appropriate, what the group is all about, how power and control will get administered, and so on. Satisfactorily solving these issues provides a foundation upon which members can stand. It allows them to feel a strong attachment to the group and to each other.

Thus the members of this group had been able to forge together a cohesion, or a common "we-ness." They experienced a palpable sense that they were involved in a mutual enterprise that they were creating and about which they possessed positive feelings.

One of the signs of cohesion is that members not only interact more freely and less guardedly, but that the quality of their interaction deepens. This depth is often tied to more frequent and riskier levels of self-disclosure and feedback. These two processes are fundamentally important to effective group work.

Self-disclosure in groups involves members sharing something about themselves that is personally meaningful, something that they probably would not share in ordinary social situations. The content reveals the self and it usually includes some element of affect and risk. Certainly, Bill engaged in much self-disclosure in session five as he told the group about his 'hero' and 'chicken,' for instance. In order for a group experience to become helpful for its participants, they need to reveal to one another what it is that they want, need, fear, or are proud of: They must share their thoughts and feelings in such a way that others can understand and relate to them. By doing this, the self-discloser becomes better able to sort through his or her own feelings and members gain access to information that allows them to become potential helpers of one another.

Feedback is the counterpart to self-disclosure. Where, in self-disclosure I reveal something significant about me to you, in feedback I say something important about how I react to you. Feedback functions as a figurative mirror in a group. It involves member "A" telling member "B," for example, how what B just did in the group affects A. Member A holds up a "mirror" so that member B can learn the interpersonal effects of his or her behavior. The importance of feedback increases as several members share their impressions of another member's behavior so that the receiving member can get ample information and examine it for similarities and differences.

The group experience affords a unique opportunity for people to obtain this kind of interpersonal information, an opportunity that can be found in few other social situations. Along with self-disclosure, feedback is one of the critically important therapeutic processes of group life. The effect of both processes is to generate the kind of personal and interpersonal data that group members need to become mutual helpers. These vital data become available during the cohesion stage. And when the data are flowing, when members are openly engaging with each other in a climate of trust, the experience of group leading can feel genuinely rewarding.

This is the feeling that Heather and Fred were acknowledging. As coleaders of that fifth group session, they found themselves in the enviable position of trying to "catch the wave" and facilitate its progress. In a very real sense, the best strategy at times like this is for leaders not to get in the way of member momentum, or if they choose to intervene, to do so with the goal of focusing and harnessing the energy. Too many group leaders make the mistake of excessive intervention at this point. This is not the time for leaders to take charge but the time to support and guide the charging ahead of the members. Sometimes a focusing exercise can provide this effect.

"I did have the strong intuition that the pairing exercise might really help to pinpoint the movement I was seeing," said Heather as she began discussing the exercise she introduced fairly early in the preceding session. "I was relieved you thought it was OK to do, Fred, and that it actually did work."

"Me, too," agreed Fred. "You know I am not very keen on using structured exercises in groups—we've been through that before. But I was willing to trust you on this and I *really* felt good that you brought it up in the group so I knew where you wanted to go. It also occurs to me that what you did there was pretty risky—what if I didn't agree? But I was pleased you did it, that you gave me the chance to respond."

Heather responded. "It was risky! I felt out on a limb, but I thought I had to check it out with you. If you had disagreed, who knows? I probably wouldn't have liked it, but I suppose we would have worked it out somehow. And maybe going through that would have been good modeling for the group members, too. You know, that people can work out their differences."

"I think you're right, Heather. And one of the lucky things about the exercise, I think, was that Judy paired up with Bill," observed Fred. "There is just something about that relationship—something about what Judy is able to do to help Bill at least—that literally propels him on. I'm thinking that without the exercise, and the pairing that came out of it, that maybe Bill wouldn't have moved the way he did."

"I think she may provide the kind of caring that Bill doesn't have in his life at all," observed Heather. "You remember how he talked about feeling very empty and how he wants to develop friends and relationships? I remember from our screening interview with him how he talked some about this, too. I see Bill as being 'full' at the professional end of things, but as being near 'empty' at the personal end. And Judy, I'm guessing, is able to speak to that emptiness. She seems to be able to touch him where he is vulnerable but not to scare him away, either. No doubt about it. She's good at that, and he is responding. I was very impressed this week with both of them."

"Yeah, I think you are on to something there, Heather. As I listened to you just now, I became aware of something Bill said, or maybe that he didn't say. It had to do with this emptiness in his life but, more than that, I thought I heard something about wanting to find a relationship—how did he put it—like he used to have, or something . . . do you recall that?"

Heather had noted that comment. In fact, she had considered at the time picking up on it with Bill. But she had decided against it. There was something there that seemed perhaps too painful yet, something that was beginning to surface but not yet quite ready, she thought.

"Yes, I do. I'm thinking Bill is working on getting near to something in his life that is somehow very important and troubling. I almost went after it, but didn't. I didn't think it was the time. I don't know, but I do think that Bill is moving like lightning in this group now. He is really changing," concluded Heather.

"No question about that," concurred Fred. "He revealed more about himself—in fact, most members did in the session—but he went so far beyond what I ever expected he would that I am simply amazed at his progress. I sort of wish Bill were here with us now to let us know how he is feeling about all of this . . ."

BILL'S THOUGHTS

In fact, Bill left the session feeling about 1,000 pounds lighter, as if he had just shed an immense weight. He experienced himself as freer, kind of floating and reveling in a newfound sense of openness. He was ecstatic, very much pleased with his emerging self. He wished the next group session were tomorrow, not in the week-year when it actually would occur!

But time often serves to change things. He found himself at work during the week thinking about the session. At first, and for a while, his thoughts were filled with enthusiasm. He was even aware of feeling much differently while at work, much lighter and happier. He liked that change very much. But as the week wore on, Bill became aware of a gradual erosion of his positive affect about the session and his behavior in it. He was becoming aware of this slippage and he wondered why.

He took his confusion to the Moonbeam the night before the next group session. Actually, he went to his old haunt to get away from his obsessions about the group, maybe to have some fun. But it did not work. Soon he was once again analyzing what had happened and wondering what he should do in the future.

He looked around from his thoughts and saw lots of couples seated around the room. People who seemed to be enjoying each other's company, or at the very least, in company with someone else. Suddenly, it hit him squarely, the realization that he was once again alone, with no one else to talk to about his thoughts and feelings. And this aloneness, something that he had learned to take a great measure of pride in, was now beginning to feel very much like something far different. The aloneness, a former virtue, he was now viewing as loneliness, a kind of aching for intimate companionship. The kind of relationship he once had with—should he admit it, even to himself, and risk bringing up the pain all over again—Chelsea.

Maybe all the immersion in work, all the "GTs" with scores of women since then, had helped him to deny the pain of her tragic death in the car accident, had protected him from really coming to grips with all that. As he considered this possibility, his eyes blurred with tears at the realization that he was getting close to something that was very real for him. He yearned to have Chelsea back, which was impossible, of course. Maybe he should admit this to himself, face up to the games he had been playing, and begin to reach out, to take risks, to find someone else in his life. Was he ready?

Things are going just too fast here, he thought. At least too fast for me, they feel out of control, even if they are right on the money. Maybe I need to pull back some, to catch my breath. And the next session is tomorrow night! All of a sudden, I don't think I'm ready for it . . .

Chapter 15

INTERDEPENDENCE AND CLOSURE EMERGE IN THE GROUP

Sessions six and seven of this ten-session group experience had come and gone, following as they did on the heels of the very productive fifth session that Fred and Heather had just processed. They were interesting and constructive sessions, continuing the forward movement that had been established. At the same time, they lacked the intensity that had so decidedly characterized session five.

A disappointment for Heather and Fred was Bill's silence in the sixth session. After the previous session, where Bill had made such marked strides in self-disclosure, suddenly he had clammed up. Although he was there physically, he seemed not to be there as a participant. It appeared that he had thrown up a wall behind which he was hiding. And although others in the group were involved actively in the session, Bill remained on the outside looking in.

Heather had decided to confront this discrepancy between Bill's "open" and "closed" behavior in the seventh session, if the inconsistency continued. For his part, Bill wavered. He almost felt an urge to take risks and to become reinvolved. He could not bring himself to try, however. Somehow he felt frozen at an impasse and it was easier to remain quiet—and protected. He rationalized it as "letting others have time in the group," although he knew that was just a ruse.

So the seventh session came with no apparent change in Bill's behavior. About a quarter of the way through it, Heather took up the challenge. She addressed Bill directly, and pointed to what she had observed as a gap between his recent "closed" behavior and his really "open" behavior of two sessions ago. She invited Bill to talk about this:

Was her observation accurate? If so, what was going on? Could the group somehow be helpful to him?

Her bidding drew Bill back into the group. He needed someone to reach into him, to help him to climb up and over the wall he had erected. Somewhat predictably, Judy was there, too, telling him that she was wondering about the same things as Heather. She said she hoped he would once again be able to renew his involvement with the group.

With this help and support, then, Bill decided to cast aside much of his restraint and to plunge back in. Soon he asked the group members for feedback about how he came across throughout the group. Although he might not have been quite ready for all that he heard, it did seem honest to him and uncannily accurate.

Bill was told that, for a long time—but not any more—group members perceived him as obnoxious, self-centered, and a bully. At the coleaders' request, they pointed to several examples of this sort of behavior, such as the numerous times when Bill so bluntly demanded that the group and its leaders get on with the show because his time was so valuable! As well, they identified what Bill had done in the group to help change members' perceptions of him, such as his admissions of self-doubt.

His earlier rudeness was chalked up by most as a kind of "cockiness," a sense by Bill that he was better than everyone else. He needed, they thought, to learn something about humility and to realize that others, although they might be different from him, were also able and strong in their own ways.

Judy saw it differently, as she often did when it came to Bill. She suggested to him that at the root of all this blustery behavior was not a feeling of being "better than," but maybe of feeling "less than." After all, Bill himself had begun to share these kinds of feelings two sessions ago—that he was unfulfilled and feeling pretty empty, she remembered—and then he had closed down. As the seventh session closed, Bill was about ready to acknowledge her wisdom.

And now session eight was upon them, with only two to go after it. Fred and Heather opened it by drawing attention to the approaching end of the group.

Fred said, "You know, there are only two more group sessions to go following tonight's. We are fast nearing the end of this group, which really does seem unbelievable to me. What this means is that not too much time is left for you to get what you need, to reach the goals you set out for yourself earlier. We want to encourage each of you, then, to push onward tonight and next week to realize your goals here. Most important, don't slack off and coast to the end, as sometimes can be the temptation."

And then Heather picked up. "Yes, and a couple of other important things are upcoming as we approach termination of the group. We will want to be helping you to make sense of what you have done and learned during this group. We'll be working on what all this means for you. This is very important. As you may remember from when we talked individually during screening, this group is only a *means* toward ends that you want to accomplish and put into effect out there, in the 'real world' of your lives. And finally, you will want to say goodbye here before leaving, to bring a kind of closure to the whole experience—and we will try to help you do that during the final session in two weeks."

Fred tried to summarize this lecturette on the approaching termination and what it meant. "What we're trying to say here, in a nutshell, is that we are at a crucial point together. Now is the time to work hardest at your growth, because the group's end is coming quickly . . . Who wants to start?"

Despite their attempts to propel the group members forward, for the next 25 minutes the members reacted to the reality of termination. Some wondered if it was worth it to invest too much more in the group because soon they would all be parting anyway. Others began to reflect on some of the events that had occurred already, such as the first session when no one knew anyone else and how unsettling that feeling was for them. They were exploring very real phenomena related to endings. But they were also avoiding the invitation of the leaders to focus concertedly on the here and now as their time together was rapidly waning.

The surprise was that Bill changed the group's direction.

"I have been thinking about what I need to do here," said Bill, "before it's too late. I wonder if I could have some time?" he asked, looking at Heather and Fred.

Fred was quick to respond. "If it's all right with the others, going ahead seems exactly the thing to do. What do you say?" he inquired of the group members.

They nodded in agreement, and most leaned forward in interest.

"Well, I don't know," Bill began hesitatingly. "I kind of think that Judy was right last week when she was talking about my feeling empty. I mean that I think there is something about that whole area that I may need to take care of, and that's what I think I need to do here. But I'm not sure at all how to do it."

"What about the emptiness?" asked Peter, who was finding it much easier to connect with this 'new' Bill.

"I've been wondering since early in the group why I've been putting people off. I don't think I've always been that way. I also have been trying to figure out why my life has felt so driven ever since I moved out here and began the law practice. And through it all I have wound up feeling pretty alone."

Bill continued after a pause in which he seemed to be churning over some important thoughts and feelings.

"I am concluding, and this is what I think I want to share and get some feedback about, that all this is tied to something I haven't told you about. Something that happened just before I moved out here . . ."

Tears began to fill Bill's eyes as he hastened on.

"What it is, is that I've walled myself off from others and become a workaholic and a sort of one-night stand guy. I've enjoyed a whole lot of 'success' in both areas. But I just can't stand it anymore."

"Is it important that we know why all this has happened?" asked Heather.

"I don't know, but I think it's real important that I tell you, at least for me," replied Bill.

"You see, I was going to get married to somebody I loved very much." As he began this, Bill realized he had never disclosed any of this to anyone before.

"Her name was Chelsea. She was beautiful and wonderful. We had met when I was in law school and she was finishing college. Back East. I became completely enthralled by her, and I think vice versa."

His voice thickened with sadness as the memories came roaring back, and he had to rest for a few moments.

Bill continued. "Chelsea was killed in a car crash not long before our wedding date. I haven't been the same since, I don't think I've ever recovered. I've just become the kind of guy you've seen here. I've got to change so that I can get my life back together."

There, he had done it, Bill thought. And rather than feeling weak and completely exposed, he felt relieved and strangely energized. He found himself looking forward to whatever might come from the group.

What he got was unqualified support to continue what came to be called the "new Bill." He was told that he was doing in the group a whole lot of what he might want to begin doing outside the group. That is, he was encouraged to stay in touch with his feeling of incompleteness and, rather than to deny it or to cover it over through obsessive workaholism or through passing sexual relationships, to recognize his need to fill it in.

That Bill could understand. But how to "fill it in" was a big question mark for him.

Judy provided some help when he asked about it.

"Bill, all you have to do is to be yourself. I mean more the self that we have seen in the last few weeks here, and certainly tonight, than who you presented at the start. I respond to you completely differently—much more positively—when you show some feeling, when you open up to others more. And I think others have here, too."

Several other members agreed with Judy. And Bill was helped to identify some more specific behaviors he could apply outside the group.

The last two group sessions continued in this vein. Members worked interdependently, asking for and receiving help. In a very real way, this group had become a mutual helping system characterized by the constructive give-and-take of assistance.

As the last session, the termination, came it was the final chance to consolidate any learnings attained, and to bid goodbye to one another. Heather and Fred worked very hard in this concluding session to assist the members to attribute meaning to important events, to link the meaning with translation to their "real world," and to be as sure as possible that no significant "unfinished business" remained.

As one part of this last session, and toward its end, the coleaders asked the members to complete a brief group evaluation form. Following that, they took 15 minutes to discuss how effective the group had been and what recommendations they might have for improvement. Among other things, they learned that members felt rushed in the 10-week period. Where at first 10 weeks seemed like a tremendously long period of time, once they got into the experience, it proved to be too short for several. Most of what was shared testified to the helpfulness of each other in the process, and not just of the leaders. They seemed to find that unexpected. Most had found the experience considerably more powerful and useful than they had expected. Finally, it emerged that all members were interested in a group follow-up session that was proposed by Heather and Fred. They decided to hold it in six weeks at the Y. It would be a time when they could "reconnect" and talk about what each had been able to put into practice since the group had ended.

With that "business" transacted, time had expired. The group was over but, for members such as Bill, the adventure was only just beginning.

Chapter 16

PROCESSING INTERDEPENDENCE

FRED AND HEATHER'S FINAL THOUGHTS

When coleaders meet for the final time that, too, can bring many feelings to the fore. Endings are often difficult to cope with, especially so when a meaningful event or relationship is involved. Heather and Fred recognized this reality as they met for the last time to process their group, which had just ended the day before.

"Does it feel finished to you?" Heather asked Fred.

"Yes, I think so," Fred said. "It could have gone on longer, as some members had wished. But I feel pretty much finished with the group, in a really good way," he added. "How about you?"

"I'm feeling some sadness, I think, that the whole thing is over. A lot of connection developed there. I became involved in what was happening, and ending it all sort of leaves me dangling some. But, aside from that, I think that we ended at a good spot and that everyone had a solid chance to wrap things up," said Heather.

"Well, I'll admit to some sadness, too," admitted Fred. "That group sure did some very exciting things and some of the changes we saw happening were remarkable in just ten weeks. I really will miss getting back together again. But I'm also remembering that a reunion is coming in six weeks, and I'm looking forward to that."

"You know, I'm glad that we finally had the opportunity to colead a group," shared Heather. "It's something we've wanted to do for some time and I very much enjoyed working with you—as I thought I would. What I liked especially was our ability to 'give and take,' to be able to communicate openly, not only as we met after the group sessions but, even more so, during the sessions themselves."

"I couldn't agree more," replied Fred enthusiastically. "I think we developed a leadership style that worked well in the group and that modeled a sense of openness. And it felt very freeing and comfortable to me, which I liked very much. We must do this again sometime soon!"

"I'd like that," quickly replied Heather. "You know, we'll need to meet with Dave Hoover from the Y next week to close the group administratively. Maybe at that time we could sound him out about a future group. We also can share with him our impressions of the group and the group evaluations the members completed."

"Those group member evaluations are awfully persuasive, I'd say!" observed Fred. "How could Dave not want us to do another group?" he laughed. "I think we have a good thing going here that we should continue."

"I've been wondering all through the group what it was that was allowing it to go so well and for us to work together so effectively," said Heather. "I've come up with what I think is a very important ingredient. Want to know what it is?" teased Heather.

"You remind me of a TV spot for the 11:00 news—go ahead, you have me absolutely riveted!" joked Fred.

Heather chuckled. "OK, I think a major factor was the gobs and gobs of time and energy that we put into the preparation and planning for this group in the first place. Remember back to then?"

Fred nodded and rolled his eyes at the memory of those meetings. A lot of work had gone into them.

Heather continued. "All of that helped us to jointly develop a plan for action and forced us really to communicate. No doubt about it—we were ready to work together. I really think that we had built a strong foundation that held up throughout the group's life—and, of course, our weekly processing meetings continued it. I think if anyone were to ask me what I would recommend most for coleaders to do, based on our experience, it would be to be sure you have created a group plan and that you hammer out a way to communicate effectively."

"I agree totally," responded Fred. "Even though, at the time, I resented all the time we were putting into it. I had so many other important things to be doing then. Hey, you know, I kind of sound like the 'old Bill,' don't I?"

"Kind of," smiled Heather. "Wow, there was a remarkable change story! I guess I feel especially pleased about the progress Bill made in the group, and of how we were able to be part of that."

"I'll say!" agreed Fred. "From the 'old Bill' to the 'new Bill.' I would never have guessed it to be possible, in just 10 weeks. And, at the beginning, he seemed so belligerent, too."

"Yes, he was a resistance fighter, wasn't he!" concurred Heather. "Or so he appeared. But he really wanted, underneath all that bravado, was to soften up and change. What helped him a whole lot to take the necessary steps was Judy, don't you think? I mean she seemed somehow to connect with him, to see what he was truly struggling with . . ."

"Yes, I saw that," said Fred. "Often, and it was the case here, a group member can be the true therapeutic agent for another group member. What it was about Judy and about Bill that allowed for this to happen, I don't know. But she went after him. I saw her sometimes offering him support, sometimes she provided a needed challenge. Maybe she offered the kind of relationship that Bill had been lacking, or avoiding, ever since, who was it—Chelsea—had died. I don't know, and perhaps it isn't important that I do. The critical thing, it seems to me, is that something powerfully positive happened between them to enable Bill really to advance, almost to blow right through his psychological blockage. It was amazing to behold!"

Fred and Heather closed their last processing session shortly, feeling satisfied about their group's accomplishments and determined to initiate another group. They also hoped that the members, such as Bill, would be able to carry forward whatever learnings they had gained in the group to their daily lives.

BILL'S FINAL THOUGHTS

It was over. What a relief, he thought.

No more "cranking up" for those Thursday night group sessions. No more having to push himself to go or to be involved. No more of being almost forced to analyze himself between those sessions, either. He was free of that pressure, and it felt like none too soon.

Bill was at the Moonbeam the Friday night following the last group session of the night before. He went to have a good time, to sort of celebrate the ending of the group, the beginning of something else. What that "something else" was, he didn't know. Right now it simply felt like the removal of a large burden from his shoulders—the group was over and he could return to being himself.

But Bill no longer knew what "being himself" meant. In a very real way, it seemed to mean not being himself—or being his true self. Or something.

Whatever it was, he was feeling different. What had begun as a toast to his newfound freedom from the group he was now recognizing as a tribute to his new self. To what in the group had become known as the "new Bill." He began to get in touch with a feeling of elation. It reminded him somewhat of the turnabout of Scrooge in Dickens's *A Christmas*

Carol. What he had begun to become aware of during the latter stages of the group was continuing now that the group had ended. This was exciting!

Bill was seeing himself and the world through new eyes. He remembered Judy's words to him during the last group session: "I respond to you completely differently—much more positively—when you show more feeling, when you open up to others more," she had said.

Suddenly, as he sat there in the noisy bar, he realized what he had to do. He could not put the group experience behind him, all wrapped up in a bow and done with. What he had learned about himself, and others, was now very much a part of him. He needed to incorporate these gains and to act accordingly. Opening himself up to others, as Judy had observed, was what he needed to do. Taking some risks. Attending to feeling. Becoming a more complete human being. And, in the process, maybe finding another woman who could help fill the void left in his life by Chelsea's untimely death. He was beginning to think he was ready to try.

Perhaps, he thought, the Moonbeam, as much as he liked it, was not the sort of setting to work on these kinds of goals. At least not for right now.

It was time for him to move on. Bill left the bar, feeling upbeat and clear-headed about his life direction.

REFLECTIONS AND ACTIVITIES:
PERSONAL GROUP

As was the "Reflections and Activities" material following Part I, this material is intended for students and trainees who are reading this book as part of an educational or training experience, such as a course or workshop. However, I hope it will be interesting and useful to other readers, too, such as practitioners who are out in the trenches right now.

1.   Coleadership of a personal group can be a wonderful experience for the leaders, or it can be a nightmare. Why is that the case? What did you see Heather and Fred doing that seemed positive? What similarities and differences do you think exist between coleadership and solo leadership?

2.   Have you ever been at a point of deciding whether to join a personal growth group? If so, what thoughts and feelings did you have? If not, what do you imagine this could be like for you? What do you make of Bill Johnson's approach to this and his experience of reaching a decision?

3. From time to time in the group, conflict emerged. Pick out one instance and discuss it with a partner. How was it handled? How do you think each of you would have handled it? How able are you to cope with conflict?

4. What did you make of the leadership styles of Fred and Heather? How would you describe them? How similar or dissimilar were they to how you are (or might be, if you have not had this experience yet) as a leader of a group such as this one?

5. Form a group of five to eight peers. Select a group leader for this exercise. Interact for 20 minutes about three things you most liked about what the coleaders of the "Personal Growth Group for Professionals" did in the group and three things you liked least about what they did. Spend 10 minutes after this experience discussing the process of your interaction.

6. Trace the group developmental stages that the personal growth group for professionals went through in the book. Discuss these with a partner. Identify a specific event that occurred in each stage.

7. Why might it be useful for a personal group leader to know something about group developmental stages?

8. Describe the evolution that Bill seemed to go through during the group. What do you make of it? Does it seem realistic? Or is it not really possible for this kind of change to happen in just a few weeks of work in a group like that?

9. What is it like for you to be a member of a group such as the one described in this part of the book? Or, if you have not yet been involved in such an experience, what would you imagine your reactions to be? How comfortable? How energized? How defensive? Discuss your reflections with a peer.

10. How effective a leader of a personal group are you right now or, if you have not yet done this, how effective do you think you might be? In what areas might you want to develop?

PART III

Conceptual Framework

This last section of the book contains Chapter 17. It departs from the alternating story and analysis format of the book. This chapter provides a discussion of the basic conceptual framework underlying the task group ("Committee on Social Responsibility") and the personal group ("Personal Growth Group for Professionals") that are the foci of the book.

Integrating this conceptual material with the practical information of the preceding chapters should result in a more complete understanding of groups and how to work with them.

Chapter 17

SOME EXPLANATORY AND CONCEPTUAL SUPPORTS

EXPLANATION

This chapter is unlike any of the preceding 16. Rather than contributing to the telling of an ongoing story—whether it be the church "Committee on Social Responsibility" of Chapters 1 through 8, or the "Personal Growth Group for Professionals" of Chapters 9 through 16—this chapter contains supportive explanatory and conceptual material. It is meant to provide a framework within which the two stories can be understood. Moreover, it is intended to assist readers to understand and lead groups of their own more effectively.

One of the important findings about groups that has emerged in the research literature (Lieberman, Yalom, & Miles, 1973) is the immensely positive contribution of a leadership function called *meaning attribution*. This function is applied when group leaders help members to make cognitive sense of the experience in which they were just involved. A frequent criticism of group work, especially group work of a personal nature, has been that members may participate in many seemingly consequential experiences without learning sufficiently what they mean, why they occurred, or how principles drawn from the experience could be applied elsewhere. An abbreviated version of this dilemma was the title of a useful book in the field, *After the Turn-On, What?* (Houts & Serber, 1972). I hope in this chapter to avoid this pitfall. The material presented is intended to help readers attribute meaning to the two group experiences described throughout the book.

It may not matter whether the reader starts or ends with this chapter. Perhaps doing both would be suitable. The chapter is presented to provide both an orientation and a summation for the ongoing stories about the two groups.

The two "stories" illustrate two different common forms of group work: a *task* group (the committee) and a *personal* group (the growth group for professionals). A task group and a personal growth group were chosen because they reflect well the major ways in which groups are used in this culture to accomplish goals. For instance, task groups proliferate, from committees of all kinds to study circles, to the literally thousands and thousands of meetings occurring every day across the land. As well, personal groups also are a preferred vehicle for providing personal and interpersonal support and for the delivery of counseling, psychotherapy, and other forms of help-giving. No matter how the subject is considered, groups are used extensively now and they can only be expected to increase in the future. Therefore, I believe that professionals engaged in contemporary group work need to be prepared to exercise their competencies in both the personal and the task group domains (Conyne, 1982, 1985a, 1985b).

The two stories in this book seek to highlight relevant events of the group being considered from the perspective of both the group leader(s) and one or more group members. Dealing with the unfolding group circumstances from leader and member positions is meant to afford a unique vantage point about how groups can function. In addition, the alternating "processing" chapters, which present the leader(s) engaging in various forms of reflection and planning about their group, are meant to lead the reader to contemplate the foregoing events and to place them in perspective. By so alternating group session discussions with group processing analyses, I have sought to reinforce the concept of "meaning attribution" that was discussed above.

RELATED CONCEPTUAL SUPPORTS

Group work can be a bewildering experience. I think it is one of the more complex activities with which a professional helper—counselor or consultant, for example—can become involved.

This is the case because so much is occurring all the time in groups. Let's take just two examples. Three group members may interact energetically for 15 minutes or so. They may cover a range of topics, expressing a variety of thoughts and feelings.

How does one make sense of *what* is being said, or of what is not being said? These are questions of content, that is, the subjects of discussion. As Hill (1965) has observed in his very useful Hill Interaction Matrix (HIM), these content subjects can include "nonpersonal matters" (e.g., external topics, such as the weather) and "group matters" (e.g., discussions about the group itself without reference to individuals in it). Another source of complexity is *how* group members are verbally interacting. Again, according to Hill, group members can discuss group subjects in a relatively safe and "preworking" way (e.g., in a conventional, social chit-chat approach) or in a highly risky, "working" manner (e.g., engaging in direct confrontation with each other). In addition, each form of what-how verbal interaction is thought to hold therapeutic value, depending on when it may occur during the developmental life span of the group.

It is this concept of group "developmental life span" that I have selected as a guiding framework for the group sessions that evolve in this book. As a group leader, whether that may be of a task committee or of a psychotherapy group, one needs to operate from an effective and appropriate organizing framework. Failing to do so will lead inevitably to an inability to recognize and process relevant information and it will prevent the leader from anticipating what may be likely to happen in the group. I have found organizing frameworks, such as the HIM I mentioned above about verbal interaction patterns, and group developmental life span models, to be helpful particularly in sorting out and anticipating group events.

Well over 100 group developmental life span models are available for consideration (Forsyth, 1983). These models can be arranged into *recurring-phase* or into *sequential-stage approaches.*

Schutz (1958) provided an example of the recurring-phase approach in his Fundamental Interpersonal Relations Orientation-Behavior (FIRO-B) model. He discussed the stages of inclusion (being "in" or "out" of the group), control (being "on top" or "on the bottom" in the group), and openness (being "near" or "far" in the group) as representing a logical developmental sequence, which reverses itself as a group approaches termination.

Tuckman and Jensen (1977) offered an illustration of the sequential-stage approach. They discussed the progression in a group as being characterized by stages of forming (getting oriented), storming (conflict), norming (cohesiveness), performing (problem solving), and adjourning (termination). In another parallel model, Anderson (1984) organized the developmental stage sequence as trust, autonomy, closeness, interdependence, and termination (producing the acronym "TACIT").

Any of these models cited, or many of the other available ones, can be useful to the group leader by providing a conceptual road map for understanding and predicting group events. I believe the really important

TABLE 17.1   Task-Personal Stage Model

Stage	Personal Relations	Task Functions
1	dependency	orientation
2	conflict	organization
3	cohesion	data-flow
4	interdependence	problem solving

SOURCE: Reprinted from J. William Pfeiffer and John E. Jones (Eds.), *The 1973 Annual Handbook for Group Facilitators*, San Diego, CA: University Associates, Inc., 1973. Used with permission.

thing is to select a model that fits one's style and working situation and then to use it in a flexible way to assist in alleviating the unnecessary confusion that faces any group leader.

The Task-Personal Stage Model. The group developmental life span model followed throughout the two groups described in this book was presented by Jones (1973). The particular value of this model, which I call the "task-personal stage model," is that it gives specific attention to both *task* and *personal* stages in group evolution. The model holds that in any group, regardless of whether it may be a task group or a personal group, attention must be given to *both* personal and task processes. The components of the task-personal stage model (Jones, 1973, p. 129) are shown in Table 17.1.

A brief description of the four stages of this model would be helpful to apply to the ongoing task and personal group examples presented in this book. In stage one, the beginning of any group's life, group members must resolve a number of personal relations having to do with *dependency*. They tend to rely heavily on the designated leader at that point for direction. Simultaneously, in terms of task functions, members require an *orientation* to the purpose of the group and development of an understanding of what they are to do together.

In stage two, *conflict* characterizes the personal relations among members. This conflict may be overt or covert. Yet it has to do with jockeying for position, who has power, how authority considerations will get resolved. With regard to task functions, the group members are concerned with the *organization* of work and how it will get done.

Questions include who will do what, what procedures will be used, and what time lines will be in effect.

Stage three of this model finds personal relations to be focused on *cohesion*. Assuming the group gets to this point, members become aware of developing a sense of "we-ness." They have grappled successfully with challenges of the earlier two stages to arrive at a closeness that is palpable. It now becomes possible for task functions to be dominated by *data-flow*. Ideas and feelings are shared and reacted to more openly and with a *sense of freedom*.

Finally, stage four may be arrived at by some groups. On the personal relations end, stage four is typified by *interdependence*. That is, group members can work in any variety of combinations. They can function well individually, in subgroups, or as a totality. They can compete and collaborate. They can think, act, and feel together as the situation warrants. This organicity allows the opportunity for *problem solving* on the task functions side. Data that are produced can now be processed to conclusion, there exists a strong commitment to working together to arrive at solutions, and high-quality end products tend to result from common activity.

Although Jones did not specify it in this model, I must point out that it is also in stage four that group termination needs to be planned for and accomplished. Termination involves a number of important considerations, including helping members to develop a sense of task completion, preparing them to say goodbye to one another, and giving attention to learnings derived from the experience that can be translated and applied to settings outside the group.

It has been pointed out that any group, whether task or personal in emphasis, must concern itself with all aspects of the model just presented. In practice, however, it is the case that personal groups are *most* concerned with the personal relations dimension of the model and task groups are *most* concerned with task functions.

To illustrate this situation, the church "Committee for Social Responsibility" (a task group), that commands the attention of Chapters 1 through 8 in this book, is considered from the perspective of task functions. The book chapters are arranged in accordance with the model: orientation, organization, data-flow, and problem solving. Likewise, the "Personal Growth Group for Professionals" (a personal group), the subject of Chapters 9 through 16, is considered from the perspective of personal relations. Therefore, consistent with the model, those book chapters are presented in this order: dependency, conflict, cohesion, and interdependence.

Of course, when actually working with any one task or personal group, it is important to remember that absolute symmetry between group developmental conceptual models and real world practice is always incomplete. While the ongoing groups described in this book reflect considerable reality, they have been somewhat artificially forced to correspond neatly to the Task-Personal Stage model. This is a pedagogical device, aimed at conveying a real understanding of how groups can evolve according to a developmental pattern. It should not be confused, however, with a specific prediction of how real world events may occur in any one group.

At the same time, this book is meant to serve the practical function of improving the understanding and practice of group work. To that end, I hope that the evolving stories and their analyses are useful.

ANNOTATED BIBLIOGRAPHY

SOME GENERAL REFERENCES ABOUT GROUP WORK

Alissi, A. (Ed.). (1980). *Perspective on social group work practice: A book of readings.* New York: Free Press.

This edited book contains 25 papers that present the full spectrum of classic and current perspectives in social group work, from history, to application, to the range of personal growth and social change approaches. Each chapter includes study questions to help students and practitioners evaluate current practice and develop an individual approach to social group work.

Bertcher, H. (1979). *Human services guide: Vol. 10. Group participation: Techniques for leaders and members* (2nd ed.). Beverly Hills, CA: Sage.

This very practical book examines the "effective group" and provides concrete information about 12 skills that are useful in producing it.

Cartwright, D., & Zander, A. (Eds.). (1968). *Group dynamics* (2nd ed.). New York: Harper & Row.

This excellent resource book provides general coverage of a broad range of subjects of interest to group workers, including group membership and leadership, motivational processes, power and influence, structural properties, and pressures to uniformity, among others. It remains a classic in the field.

Conyne, R. (Ed.). (1985). *The group workers' handbook: Varieties of group experience.* Springfield, IL: Charles C Thomas.

This book examines the broad spectrum of personal and of task groups with which group workers can become involved. Groups that target various levels—individual, group, organizational, and community—are examined through original chapters that challenge the thinking of today's group counselors.

Garvin, C. (1987). *Contemporary group work* (2nd ed.). Englewood Cliffs, NJ: Prentice-Hall.

This book is an introductory text on group work in social welfare settings. It is a broad-gauged text, adeptly covering the spectrum of personal and task groups. The author succeeds in providing a scholarly yet practical framework for working with groups today.

Glasser, P., & Mayadas, N. (Eds.). (1980). *Group workers at work: Theory and practice in the '80's*. Totowa, NJ: Rowman & Littlefield.

This edited book of 21 papers reflects the hope of its editors that social group work return to its leadership role in the social work profession. The papers effectively trace traditional themes and current directions.

Johnson, D., & Johnson, F. (1982). *Joining together: Group theory and group skills* (2nd ed.). Englewood Cliffs, NJ: Prentice-Hall.

This book creatively combines theory and experiential activities to provide an effective presentation of group dynamics and usable group skills. The material contained is widely applicable to all varieties of groups, from personal growth to task groups.

Knowles, M., & Knowles, H. (1972). *Introduction to group dynamics: What it is, its main ideas, its languages, its applications* (2nd ed.). Chicago: Follett.

This small nugget of a book is chock-full of useful information about group dynamics, with transferability to many contexts.

Luft, J. (1984). *Group processes: An introduction to group dynamics* (3rd ed.). Palo Alto, CA: Mayfield.

This classic book presents a review of traditional and recent knowledge in group dynamics and relates it to the study of interpersonal and group behavior. The material covered is pertinent to theorists, researchers, and practitioners who are involved in any way with group processes.

Napier, R., & Gershenfeld, M. (1983). *Making groups work: A guide for group leaders*. Boston: Houghton Mifflin.

This book attempts to help leaders of various kinds of groups learn how to design their groups and to capture their dynamics in such a way as to produce highly effective experiences.

Thelen, H. (1954). *Dynamics of groups at work*. Chicago: University of Chicago Press.

This enduring book is a treatise on how groups can assist individuals to cope with personal problems and how communities can try to create an improved state of affairs.

SOME PERSONAL GROUP REFERENCES

Anderson, J. (1984). *Counseling through group process*. New York: Springer.

This book presents the "TACIT" developmental model (trust, autonomy, closeness, interdependence, termination) to group counseling and illustrates its usefulness for group leaders.

Brown, A. (1986). *Groupwork* (2nd ed.). Brookfield, VT: Gower.

This primer deftly addresses several main ingredients in group work practice, including general concepts, planning a group, leadership, group process, and developing/evaluating group work skills.

Corey, G. (1985). *Theory and practice of group counseling* (2nd ed.). Monterey, CA: Brooks/Cole.

This text examines major theoretical approaches to group counseling, as well as leadership, ethics, and application issues. It is highly readable.

Corey, G., & Corey, M. (1987). *Groups: Process and practice* (3rd ed.). Monterey, CA: Brooks/Cole.

This book identifies some basic issues and important concepts of the group counseling process and shows how group leaders can apply them in their work with a range of groups. A hallmark of this book is its practicality and its "hands-on" treatment.

Gazda, G. (Ed.). (1983). *Basic approaches to group psychotherapy and group counseling* (3rd ed.). Springfield, IL: Charles C Thomas.

This comprehensive text contains considerable historical material about the field and original chapters on major theoretical approaches to group psychotherapy and group counseling. Attention is given to research effectiveness and ethics, as well.

Gazda, G. (1984). *Group counseling: A developmental approach* (3rd ed.). Boston: Allyn & Bacon.

This book approaches group counseling from a clearly drawn developmental perspective. Specific attention is given to applications with children, preadolescents, adolescents, adults and to substance abusers, families, and the elderly.

Glasser, P., Sarri, R., & Vinter, R. (Eds.). (1974). *Individual change through small groups*. New York: Free Press.

This edited text of 30 papers illustrates the range of ways that social group work practice can assist individuals to change. Its four sections describe the basic approach, activities of the professional group worker in the group, activities of the worker in the client's environment, and broad applications to various fields of practice.

Rose, S. (1977). *Group therapy: A behavioral approach*. Englewood Cliffs, NJ: Prentice-Hall.

This book does very well what its title suggests: It presents in a clear and organized manner a behavioral approach to group therapy. Its attention to the training of members in various behavioral change procedures is a particular strength.

Yalom, I. (1985). *The theory and practice of group psychotherapy* (3rd ed.). New York: Basic Books.

This book about group psychotherapy is built on an understanding of therapeutic factors, such as universalization and cohesion, that the author thinks are central to effective practice.

SOME TASK GROUP REFERENCES

Bouton, C., & Garth, R. (Eds.). (1983). *Learning in groups*. San Francisco, CA: Jossey-Bass.

This monograph is part of the "New Directions for Teaching and Learning" series, edited by K. Eble and J. Noonan. The original papers in this entry demonstrate how learning groups can be effectively designed and conducted to accomplish a robust set of educational goals.

Burke, W., & Beckhard, R. (Eds.). (1970). *Conference planning* (2nd ed.). La Jolla, CA: University Associates.

The brief papers in this small paperback, all written by noted authorities, lay out considerable practical information for anyone planning a conference. The attention given to group dynamics is specially noteworthy.

Craig, D. (1978). *HIP pocket guide to planning & evaluation*. Austin, TX: Learning Concepts.

This problem-solving method includes a number of group dynamic approaches, such as force-field analysis, to aid a planner, or a planning group, in arriving at decisions.

Hersey, P. (1984). *The situational leader: The other 59 minutes*. San Diego, CA: University Associates.

This handy and readable book summarizes the situational leadership model in very practical terms. It illustrates how appropriate measures of leader task and leader relationship behavior can be used in conjunction with member readiness to facilitate positive change in organizations and other work groups.

Hill, W. F. (1969). *Learning thru discussion: Guide for leaders and members of discussion groups* (2nd ed.). Beverly Hills, CA: Sage.

This manual presents a systematic group discussion method, based on group dynamics principles, that has been used widely in educational and community settings to learn and discuss material.

Schein, E. (1969). *Process consultation: Its role in organization development*. Reading, MA: Addison-Wesley.

While not a "group" book per se, this classic book about one approach to organization development illustrates nicely the important role of dynamics in many organizational change methods.

Schindler-Rainman, E., Lippitt, R., with Cole, J. (1977). *Taking your meetings out of the doldrums*. La Jolla, CA: University Associates.

This highly readable little book contains scads of useful tips and pointers that any meeting leader would do well to know and to use. It clearly demonstrates how proper use of group dynamics can serve to produce highly participatory meetings.

Tropman, J. (1980). *Effective meetings: Improving group decision-making*. Beverly Hills, CA: Sage.

This volume is Human Services Guide 17 in the Sage-University of Michigan School of Social Work series. It sets out to link effective group decision making with effective meetings and does an admirable job. This paperback is filled with a nice blend of concepts and practice that meeting leaders, and those who consult them, would find very useful.

Zander, A. (1982). *Making groups effective*. San Francisco, CA: Jossey-Bass.

This book conveys the results of group dynamics research, both current and historic, and how these findings can be applied in a host of group settings to make groups more effective. Group workers of all stripes would find the information both conceptually and practically of great value.

SOME GROUP JOURNALS

Group and Organization Studies Published quarterly by Sage, this journal contains original data-based articles, research review reports, research and evaluation studies, action reports, and critiques of research. Articles are oriented toward group facilitators, trainers, educators, consultants, and organizational managers.

Journal for Specialists in Group Work This is the official journal of the American Association for Specialists in Group Work, a division of the American Association for Counseling and Development (formerly, until 1983, the American Personnel and Guidance Association).

JSGW is published quarterly. It addresses the broad sweep of group work, with an emphasis on group counseling, and includes articles on research and practice.

Small Group Behavior Published quarterly by Sage, this journal is an international and interdisciplinary one, presenting research and theory about all types of small groups, including but not limited to therapy and treatment groups. It is described as a broadly conceived information channel for all group work professionals.

Social Work with Groups This journal is published quarterly by Haworth. Its articles are widely abstracted and indexed. It includes articles that cover the broad array of social work with groups and it is a major source of information for groups of social workers.

REFERENCES

Anderson, J. (1984). *Counseling through group process.* New York: Springer.

Conyne, R. (1982). On expanding horizons. *Journal for Specialists in Group Work, 7,* 2.

Conyne, R. (Ed.). (1985a). Critical issues in group work: Now and 2001 [Special issue]. *Journal for Specialists in Group Work, 10*(2).

Conyne, R. (1985b). (Ed.). *The group worker's handbook: Varieties of group experience.* Springfield, IL: Charles C Thomas.

Forsyth, D. (1983). *An introduction to group dynamics.* Monterey, CA: Brooks/Cole.

Hill, W. F. (1965). *HIM: Hill Interaction Matrix.* Los Angeles: University of Southern California, Youth Studies Center.

Houts, P., & Serber, M. (1972). *After the turn-on, what? Learning perspectives on humanistic groups.* Champaign, IL: Research Press.

Jones, J. (1973). A model of group development. In J. Jones & J. Pfeiffer (Eds.), *The 1973 annual handbook for group facilitators* (pp. 127-129). La Jolla, CA: University Associates.

Lieberman, M., Yalom, I., & Miles, M. (1973). *Encounter-groups: First facts.* New York: Basic Books.

Schutz, W. (1958). *FIRO: A three-dimensional theory of interpersonal behavior.* New York: Rinehart.

Tuckman, B., & Jensen, M. (1977). Stages of small group development revisited. *Group and Organizational Studies, 2,* 419-427.

ABOUT THE AUTHOR

ROBERT K. CONYNE, Ph.D., is Professor and Head of the School Psychology and Counseling Department at the University of Cincinnati. He has a long-standing professional commitment to group work. In addition to teaching and consulting in the area, he has served as Editor of the *Journal for Specialists in Group Work* (1975-1979), edited *The Group Workers' Handbook: Varieties of Group Experience* (Thomas, 1985), and contributed numerous articles to professional journals. His publications in related areas include *Environmental Assessment and Design* (with R. Clack, Praeger, 1981) and *Primary Preventive Counseling: Empowering People and Systems* (Accelerated Development, 1987).

NOTES

NOTES

NOTES

NOTES

NOTES

NOTES